COMPUTERIZING PERSONNEL SYSTEMS

A Basic Guide

Alastair Evans

INSTITUTE OF PERSONNEL MANAGEMENT

© 1986 Institute of Personnel Management

ISBN 0 85292 361 9

First published 1986

British Library Cataloguing in Publication Data

Evans, Alastair
   Computerizing personnel systems: a basic guide.
   1.   Personnel management — Data processing
   I.   Title   II.   Institute of Personnel
   Management
   658.3'0028'5   HF5549

ISBN   0-85292-361-9

Typeset by Illustrated Arts Ltd, Surrey, and
Printed in Great Britain by Dotesios Printers Ltd., Bradford-on-Avon

Contents

PART II
DIRECTORY OF SUPPLIERS OF COMPUTERIZED PERSONNEL SYSTEMS

Acknowledgements

This publication has been produced under the auspices of the IPM National Committee for Organization and Manpower Planning in conjunction with the IPM Information Services Department. The IPM acknowledges the assistance provided by Carol Harris and Michael Stanton of the National Committee for Organization and Manpower Planning and Giles Burrows of the IPM Information Services Department. The IPM also acknowledges the assistance provided in the preparation of this publication by Margo Rosenberg of Percom Ltd and Tony Ive of Foster Wheeler Energy Ltd and Fidelma McBride, Debbie Roberts and Anne Summun for typing the manuscript. The final content of the publication was determined by the IPM. Whilst every attempt has been made to ensure the accuracy of the content of the *Directory of Suppliers of Computerized Personnel Systems* in Part II of this publication, the IPM bears no responsibility for accuracy of the information contained in this section. Potential buyers are advised to contact suppliers for complete and up-to-date information about products.

Foreword

The IPM's National Committees are keenly aware of the need to assist personnel specialists to keep up-to-date in a wide range of fields of personnel work through the publication of short, practical guides. This is the latest in a series of these guides, in this case the responsibility for the publication being that of the National Committee for Organization and Manpower Planning.

The publication has its origins in a previous guide entitled *Computerizing Personnel Systems: Where to Go and How to Choose*, produced by the IPM Information Services Department in 1982. In the light of the popularity of this guide and fast moving developments in the field of computerized personnel systems, it was felt that the previous guide should be updated and extended. The first part of this guide provides a basic introduction to computing for the non-expert, describes some of the cost benefits and applications of computers to personnel work and suggests a systematic approach for introducing computing into the personnel function. The second part provides a directory of suppliers of computerized personnel packages, covering all types of computer hardware, bureaux services and specialized applications packages. Entries in the directory aim to provide information on the number of installations of a particular system, guidance on costs, some background information on suppliers and a description of each package.

Computerizing Personnel Systems is one of two related publications available from the IPM on this topic. This publication is intended as a basic guide to the introduction of computers to personnel work incorporating a non-technical review of the software packages available. The other publication is entitled *Developing a*

*Computerized Personnel System: The Management and Buyers'
Guide*, written by David Burns-Windsor from information technology consultants Brameur Limited, in association with the IPM and the Institute of Manpower Studies. This is aimed at personnel specialists who wish to develop a deeper understanding of computing, in particular where they are involved or are likely to be involved in the development of an in-house personnel system. It also incorporates a buyers' guide to personnel software packages which is more extensive and technical in nature than has been possible in this publication.

At a time when personnel functions are facing conflicting pressures to provide more manpower information whilst cutting back on administrative overhead costs, I commend *Computerizing Personnel Systems* to you, and hope that it will prove helpful in establishing a computerized personnel system appropriate to the needs of your organization.

Peter Lockwood
*Vice-President
Organization and
Manpower Planning*

PART I

INTRODUCING COMPUTERIZED PERSONNEL SYSTEMS

1 Introduction to computing

Computer systems consist of two main elements; hardware and software. The word hardware refers to the equipment necessary to carry out the computer's processing functions; software is the name given to the programs or instructions which determine how the data will be handled by the hardware.

Computer hardware consists of:

- a central processing unit of CPU (the computer itself)
- input devices, such as punched cards, paper tape and, increasingly, keyboards and visual display units (VDUs), akin to a television screen, which enable data to be passed into the CPU
- output devices, such as printers and VDUs, to print or display data processed by the CPU.

Input and output devices are sometimes also called peripherals, and the various combinations of pieces of hardware being used as the configuration. The information which computers are required to handle can take many forms, including numbers, letters, words and even pictures, but the computer itself is a collection of electronic devices only capable of handling electronic pulses. All the complex information of the real world has to be converted into a code, known as a binary code, which a computer can handle. All data to be handled by the computer is converted in the binary code into combinations of 0 or 1 which can be used to represent either an 'on' or 'off' state in the electronic circuitry. Different combinations of 0 and 1 are used to represent the data used in everyday life, such as numbers, alphabetic characters, punctuation marks or other symbols used on a keyboard.

Each component of a binary number, a 0 or a 1, is known as a 'bit' (binary digit). For example the number 25 would appear in binary notion as 11001 which would be a 5-bit number. A byte normally consists of at least 8 bits and is usually the equivalent of one alphabetical or numerical character or symbol. Whilst many computers are referred to as 8-bit machines, a number of more recent machines handle sequences of 16 or 32 bits at a time (referred to as 16-bit or 32-bit machines) making the speed at which information can be handled proportionately faster.

Central processing unit

The central processing unit or CPU of a computer has three main elements:

- a control system (or control unit)
- an arithmetic and logic unit or ALU
- a memory or store.

The *control system* can be described as the nerve centre of the computer which receives, interprets and implements the instructions supplied by the programs contained in the memory or instructions to activate input/output devices.

The *arithmetic and logic unit* contains the circuitry which enables the computer to perform calculations at high speed using binary arithmetic and to distinguish between the truth or falseness of the data, eg whether one number is larger than another.

The *main memory* (or immediate access store) contains information and instructions for processing by the CPU. These data or instructions may either come from an input device or are fetched from a back-up storage device (discussed below). The amount of available space on the main computer memory is usually quoted in terms of thousands of bytes (K bytes, where K in the computer field represents 1,024 bytes, not 1,000) and the main memory itself is often referred to as a 'Random Access Memory' (or RAM). Thus a 16K RAM is a main memory capable of holding up to 16,384 (1,024 x 16) characters, letters or symbols.

The main memory alone has limitations in the amount of data which can be processed, filed and retrieved, so a variety of storage

2

devices have been developed, referred as remote or back-up storage. Back-up storage is normally provided in one of the following ways, depending on the type of computer concerned:

- magnetic tape
- magnetic disk packs
- floppy disks (or diskettes)
- hard disks (or Winchesters).

Magnetic tape is a long-established medium for storing computerized information and consists of a reel of tape, akin to a cassette, which passes across a 'read/write head' from a feed reel to a take-up or machine reel. Information on the tape is stored electromagnetically and is held 'sequentially' (ie one piece of information follows another, as on a cassette tape). In order to access data held sequentially, it may be necessary to read the whole tape in order to find an item of data. Magnetic tape is capable of holding high volumes of data, processing it at high speeds and is a relatively cheap method of storage.

Magnetic disk packs consist of one or more flat circular discs of 14 inches diameter mounted on a central spindle akin to a stack of long-playing records. Data are normally recorded on both sides of each disk and are retrieved from the disks by means of a movable read/write head assembly, akin to the arm of a record player, which can locate and retrieve data in matters of milliseconds. This is referred to as 'random access' since, unlike sequential access, it is possible to go immediately to any item of data. Standard size disk packs are usually exchangeable, although very large disk packs of around 30 inches in diameter which are continually in use for a specific operation are fixed.

Floppy disks, or diskettes, have been developed for use with microcomputers and word processors. They come in three sizes, 3½, 5¼ and 8 inch diameters, in a protective paper or plastic sleeve, rather akin to a single record. Data are contained on the grooves of the disk and are read by means of an electronic pick-up arm across a window in the outer sleeve. Floppy disks normally have a storage capacity of between 300,000 to 1,000,000 bytes (or 1 megabyte). A lack of standardization in the manufacture of floppy disks has created difficulties in their interchangeability between one make of machine and another. These relate to the variation in sizes of disks, although 5½-inch disks are most common, and to the variations in disk operat-

3

ing systems (DOS) which enable the computer to understand what is contained on the disk. There are at present a small number of leading disk operating systems and it is not clear which disk operating systems will emerge as dominant in the marketplace. (Operating systems are further discussed in the section on page 10).

Hard disks, also known as Winchesters after the IBM research project which developed them, represent a further development of disk technology. Floppy disks, unlike magnetic disk packs, are not completely enclosed and protected from the environment, with the result that there can be occasional failures due to atmospheric conditions. A hard disk is a completely enclosed unit consisting of single or multiple disks available in three sizes: 5¼, 8 or 14 inch diameter. Apart from being fully protected from the environment, hard disks have a much higher storage capacity than floppy disks (up to 80 million bytes, ie 80 megabytes or over) and will work several times faster.

Magnetic tape and disk packs are usually associated with larger computers, such as mainframes and minis, and floppy and hard disks with minis and microcomputers. Typically, microcomputers have a main or random access memory of between 48 and 512K bytes with a back-up storage of between 300 to 1,000K bytes (or one megabyte) per floppy disk or up to 20,000K bytes (or 20 megabytes) using a Winchester hard disk. The capacities of minicomputers vary widely, but can be found with a main memory of between 64K bytes and 8 megabytes and a back-up storage of between 5 and 2,000 megabytes (or 2 'gigabytes').

Input devices

Inputs of data to a computer may be either direct or indirect. Direct methods, which have become increasingly common, involve input of data in the form in which it originates, via a keyboard connected directly to the computer. Keyboard terminals encode data in a form which can be understood by the computer without the need for any intermediate coding by other means. Indirect input methods require data to be converted into a format understood by the computer by means of punched cards or paper tape, and magnetic tape as described above.

Direct input methods via keyboard and visual display unit (VDU) have proliferated during the 1970s and are now the dominant form of computer input. Most VDU screens measure 12 inches diagonally, allow 80 character positions across the screen and approximately 24 lines of print. Increasingly also screen displays are available in a variety of colours. Most keyboards are laid out in the conventional QWERTY format, with additional function keys programmed so as to save the user having to type out standard instructions repeatedly, and cursor keys to indicate which item of data on the screen is to be processed. Keyboards are either attached directly to the screen or, more usually and desirably, attached only by a flexible cord, which enables the operator to place the screen and keyboard in a range of positions according to preference.

Apart from magnetic tape, other indirect methods of input have become less common, but need to be considered briefly. *Punched cards* are one medium for converting data into a form understandable by the computer. Key punch machines are used to convert information typed from a conventional typewriter keyboard into patterns of holes on the card. Following verification for accuracy, the punch cards are passed through a card reader to form computer input. *Paper tape* is similar in principle to punched cards and involves punching holes on to a role of tape by means of perforating typewriters. The tape is then passed through to a tape reader for computer input.

Output devices

The most common output devices are VDU screens for displaying data and printers for reproducing data output. Printers fall into two categories: impact and non-impact, depending on whether they incorporate a type head which strikes the paper.

The main impact printers in use are referred to as the dot-matrix and the daisy wheel. The dot-matrix printer does not have a separate printing head for each character, instead the characters are formed by a vertical set of needles which are fired at the ribbon. The daisy wheel printer resembles a golf ball type-head on which the characters are embossed on a series of plastic spokes radiating out in a circle, thus akin to a daisy in appearance. Each type of printer has its respective advantages and disadvantages and will tend to be used for different purposes. The dot-matrix printer is very much the faster of the two, with a printing speed of between 80 and 200 characters per second (cps), about one minute for a page of A4 typing. On the other hand,

5

because the print appears in the form of closely-joined dots to form the characters, it is not usually considered appropriate for high quality typed output. Dot-matrix printers tend to be used for invoices and certain internal correspondence. Daisy wheel printers are much slower, in the range of 15 to 75 cps, but because of the higher quality of print tend to be preferred for more important internal correspondence, such as reports, and for external correspondence.

Non-impact printers utilize various alternative forms of printing technology, including ink jet printers which spray a jet of ink to form the character, thermal printers which form the characters on heat sensitive paper, and laser printers which burn letters on to a page.

Types of computer

Computers are conventionally categorizsed into three broad types, although rapid technological advances over the last 10 years or so have gradually eroded some of these distinctions. The main categories are:

- mainframe computers
- minicomputers
- microcomputers.

The main differences between these computers relate to their physical size, their capabilities in terms of the speed and quantity of data processed, the number of users which they can support, the amount of data which can be stored and their cost.

Mainframe computers
Mainframe computers were the first computers to be commercially developed in the 1950s. Because of their high cost, they are generally used to provide a centrally-based computing service for the whole organization and are operated on a 24-hour basis. Mainframe computers need to be located and operated under strictly controlled environmental conditions to ensure that the atmosphere is dust-free and air-conditioned. Although all mainframes are large computers, their physical size has been reduced in recent years through the application of microelectronic circuitry. The term 'mainframe' covers a wide range of sizes and capacities of computers generally reckoned to be in the price bracket of £150,000 upwards. Apart from being expensive in

capital outlay, they require full-time operations and software support staff.

Perhaps the main change to have taken place in the use of mainframe computers in recent years is the change from the batch processing mode of operation to real time or on-line processing. Under the batch mode, work is sent to the computer centre (or bureau) where it is converted for input into the computer, typically by means of punch cards, processed at set times according to various priorities established by the organization, and returned to the user department in the form of print-outs. The main disadvantage to the user of this form of processing is the time lag which occurs and the fact that the data provided is neither instantaneous nor completely up-to-date. Increasingly this problem is being overcome by providing real time access to the computer, with input being made by the end user by means of a terminal, and frequently also a VDU, either directly or to a remote computer via a telephone line. The latter requires the use of a modem (modulator/demodulator), available from British Telecom, at each end of the line in order to convert the digital form of computer data into modulations suitable for telephone lines. Where more than one screen or keyboard will be sharing one line, a device known as a multiplexor will also be required.

Minicomputers

Minicomputers were developed in the early 1970s to meet a number of gaps in the market left by mainframes. In particular, they are aimed at the business user who wants in-house computing facilities, but has no need of or cannot afford a mainframe computer. They are also aimed at larger organizations who wish to disperse their computing facilities and place more control of computing in the hands of user departments. Minicomputers are physically smaller than mainframes, about the size of an upright filing cabinet, but nevertheless have a powerful storage and processing capacity. They are much cheaper than mainframes and, although estimating cost is difficult because of the variety of systems available, many minicomputer systems can be purchased in the price range of £30,000 to £80,000.

Whilst mainframe computers are normally used to process data for a range of user departments in medium to larger organizations, minicomputers offer an alternative approach by enabling user departments to carry out their own data processing, an approach often referred to as a dedicated system. In principle, minicomputers, unlike mainframes, do not require any specially controlled environmental conditions for their operation nor do they need the expertise of specially trained computer staff to operate them. In practice, they can generate a degree of heat and noise and should be located ideally in a separate room with extracting fans or air conditioning.

A dedicated minicomputer system is capable of processing large volumes of data and is also capable of supporting a large number of data imput terminals, on some systems in excess of 100.

Microcomputers

Microcomputers, based on the silicon chip, are a further development in the miniaturization of computers which emerged in the 1970s and are making rapid advances in sophistication and capability. At the heart of a microcomputer is a microprocessor, a silicon chip acting as the central processing unit. The programs for different operations are also on chips and programs can be easily changed by replacing one memory chip for another, making microcomputers highly flexible and adaptable. Microcomputers do not need any special environmental conditions or computer expertise to operate and can be placed on the desk top or carried from office to office. The differences in capability between the mini and the micro are becoming increasingly blurred as microcomputers become rapidly more sophisticated. The market for microcomputers is not homogeneous in nature and includes home computers, personal computers and microcomputers for business applications.

The main differences between mini- and microcomputers relate to the number of users which can be supported, the amount of data which can be stored, the time taken to process data and the capability of the micro to handle highly complex enquiries. Some microcomputers are single user systems, that is they may only be accessed through a single VDU screen. However, technology is developing fast in this field and a number of microcomputer systems on the market are capable of supporting up to a dozen terminals. A further development involves clustering or networking a number of micros in an integrated system which can be capable of supporting up to 20 users.

The cost of hardware for a fairly standard microcomputer configuration is likely to fall in the range of £5,000 to £10,000.

Software

Software is the name given to the programs which determine the way in which the hardware will operate. Without it, the hardware cannot function and indeed the quality of programming will also affect the efficiency with which the hardware does its job. Programs which control the operations of the computer itself and its peripheral devices are known as systems software and programs which manipulate data according to the requirements of the end user, eg personnel, are referred to as applications software. Applications software may be specially written to meet the specified needs of the end user, such software often being referred to as custom-built, tailor-made or bespoke systems. Applications software written for a broad range of users in different organizations is often referred to as being ready-made or packaged software.

The short discussion of software set out below is included for the general information of the reader, but it should be stressed that, for the vast majority of people using computers at work, knowledge of programming techniques as such is not necessary. Modern applications programmes enable users to access the database, retrieve, alter and manipulate data on the basis of a certain amount of training and the inputting of simple instructions into the computer.

Programming languages

Programming may be seen at a number of levels. The most fundamental program is written in machine code, with binary digits providing the basic instructions, and is referred to as the system or operating software (see below). These are prepared by the programming staff (systems programmers) employed by the computer manufacturer and provide basic instructions to the computer in relation to logical sequences, operating peripherals and applications programmes which will be subsequently added by users. System or operating software represents the basic software supplied by the manufacturer with the computer, it is kept permanently in store and is generally not accessible to users. Originally, all computer programming was carried out in machine code and was a lengthy and time-consuming process. Subsequently, low level languages, such as ASSEMBLER, were developed using mnemonics in order to convert instructions into machine code, but using these was still very time-consuming. Of most interest to those concerned with developing applications programs are high level languages such as COBOL (Common Business Oriented Language) and FORTRAN (Formula Translation) which compile more directly and readily into machine code. The most recent development is the very high level or fourth generation language which enables relatively simple instructions to be fed into and understood by the computer.

Operating systems

Lay computer users do not need to understand the complexities of systems, software or operating systems, but they do need to understand the implications of operating systems in relation to the compatibility of software, in particular software packages and computer hardware. Applications programmes, eg a personnel information system, set out the tasks to be performed by the computer and are written so that the tasks to be performed will be understood by a particular operating system within the computer. Different brands or models of computer run under different operating systems and it is not possible, for example, to run a personnel software package designed to run under one operating system on another operating system. The best analogy for this is the the video cassette recorder: if a VCR incorporates a VHS operating system, it will not function using a Betamax video cassette tape. Thus, with computers, if an organization already possesses a particular model of computer and is looking for a personnel management package to run on it, the choice will be limited to the packages available to run under that computer's operating system. It is possible that no package will be available and it is for this reason that decisions on software should precede those on hardware.

Information on the operating systems for which personnel packages are available is given in the *Directory* in Part II of this book and the potential computer user will quickly become familiar with some of the more widely-used operating systems, eg MS-DOS, PC-DOS, M/PM, CP/M, CP/M8O, UNIX, XENIX, when investigating the software packages available.

Software houses and packages

Software houses exist to provide programming expertise which is either not available in-house or where there are insufficient programming resources or expertise available in-house to carry out the necessary work. As will be discussed in Chapter 5, developing programmes in-house can be long and time-consuming, and may not always produce a satisfactory outcome, with the result that using a software house may be more cost effective. Software houses cover a wide range of specialist computer applications and may either develop software tailor-made to the specifications of the client or produce ready-made packages for specific applications or do both of these. Where software houses are producing ready-made packages only, they are usually able to offer a certain amount of customization in order to adapt standard packages to clients' specific needs. Packages have the advantage that they save the user expensive development costs, but the disadvantage that they might not fully meet all the user's needs.

2 Why computerize personnel records?

This chapter briefly considers some of the shortcomings inherent in manual personnel records systems and goes on to consider some of the potential benefits to be gained from developing a computerized personnel system. The checklists of points set out below are intended to give general guidance to personnel departments when evaluating and justifying the cost of a computerized personnel system. When putting proposals for computerization, personnel departments might usefully also consider other specific difficulties or constraints arising out of manual record keeping in the context of their own organizations.

Shortcomings of manual records systems

Cost
The work of the personnel department includes a significant clerical and routine administrative work load. The maintenance and updating of manual records systems is a labour intensive and costly process. In addition, personnel departments are frequently involved in the issuing of relatively standardized documentation, eg letters of appointment or contracts of employment, a number of which may have to be produced separately because of minor differences in the terms offered to different individuals.

Accuracy
The manual transfer of data from one record to another increases

the chance of error and, in consequence, this adversely affects the accuracy and reliability of data held.

Fragmentation

Manually stored information is frequently held in a fragmented way, with different pieces of information about employees being held in different files. Even where attempts are made to maintain comprehensive manual files on each employee, it is likely that certain items of information, such as attendance, sick pay, holidays, accident records and earnings in the year to date, will be kept in different places. Thus, many manual systems are unable to provide a single, comprehensive picture of an employee on one record.

Duplication

Manual records systems tend to be prone to duplicaton since some of the information held within the personnel records system may be needed simultaneously by a number of other departments. Thus wages offices and training departments for example may keep duplicate records to meet their specific needs. Apart from adding to the problem of fragmentation, the duplication of records further adds to costs.

Difficulty of analysis

Probably the most significant criticism of a manual records system is the difficulty presented when attempting to analyse the information held as an aid to decision-making. The manual analysis of data is extremely time-consuming and the statistical output of the personnel department tends to be limited to what can be put together more readily. The response to *ad hoc* requests for information is likely to be at best very slow and at worst completely beyond the resources of the personnel department, because staff are not available to carry out the work. Alternatively, personnel departments may attempt to improve their abilities to respond to requests for information by carrying out a range of analyses just in case they are needed, without being sure whether the time invested will actually satisfy specific requests for information. As a result of the difficulties of extracting information promptly from manual systems, the personnel function may be overlooked or bypassed as a source of useful information for decision-making and the opportunities for the personnel function to influence decisions consequently reduced.

Potential benefits of computerized personnel systems

Whilst it would be wrong to assume that computerization will automatically solve all the problems associated with manual systems, it does present a number of potential benefits which are summarized below.

Cost effectiveness
The computerization of personnel records offers an option to be considered when personnel functions are facing conflicting pressures to provide more information whilst at the same time cut back on administrative overhead costs. As the costs of computer hardware fall relative to the costs of employing clerical staff, so the adoption of computerized systems is becoming increasingly cost effective.

The extent to which the staffing costs of administering a personnel department can be reduced through computerization is not readily measurable, although one American study cites the following examples:

- a reduction of one-third in the time taken to process new employees
- savings of between 55 and 90 per cent of the time taken to provide routine information by manual methods
- clerical savings of over 600 hours per year in providing data to payroll, over 800 hours per year in preparing weekly reports and almost 500 hours per year in preparing monthly, quarterly and annual reports.[1]

One study in Britain of the application of computers to the administration of recruitment has suggested that they can speed up the administration in that area by a factor of 10. The same study also concludes that computerizing 'can bring about a very substantial reduction in the administration costs of running a personnel department and, while reducing these costs, can streamline the whole administrative operation'.[2]

It is generally accepted, however, that looking for immediate or

---

[1] TETZ TF, Evaluating computer-based human resource information systems: costs v benefits. *Personnel Journal*, June 1973, pp 451–455

[2] IVE Tony, Why Computerize?, in PAGE T. (ed) *Computers in Personnel: Making Manpower Profitable*, IMS/IPM, 1984, pp 77–82

short term cost savings reflects a highly restricted view of the potential benefits of computerization. Straight comparisons between the costs of a manually-operated system and a computerized system represent a false analogy since the computer is capable of performing a fundamentally different job. In particular, it is capable of responding quickly and accurately to many more requests for information. Thus, any adequate analysis of the cost benefits of computerization would need to take into account the improvement in the quality of human resource decision-making which is made possible, although these benefits may not be readily measurable in cost terms.

Effective human resource information
Probably more significant than its contribution to cuts in overhead costs is the potential provided by computerization for establishing an effective human resource information system. Retrieving information from manual systems is slow and cumbersome, with the result that personnel functions may be bypassed as a source of information for decision-making. It is a well worn but eminently supportable adage that 'information is power': those who wish to influence policies and decisions must be in a position to offer relevant information promptly, as and when required. A computerized personnel system, by enabling data to be readily manipulated, merged and disaggregated in response to *ad hoc* enquiries for information, will help to place personnel functions more firmly into the business of influencing policy. This potential for a change in the role of personnel functions is born out by a number of case studies. In describing the experience of computerization in the personnel department of Safeways Foodstores, John Dickie describes how the standing of the department within the company improved because it was no longer seen as 'purely an administrative function', but was increasingly viewed as 'a provider of information in the true sense of the word'.[3] In another case study of Foster Wheeler Energy, Tony Ive concludes that, apart from improving the efficiency of the personnel department, computerization is 'fundamental to the task of improving the credibility of the personnel function and extending the role which personnel departments are able to play within the organizations which they serve'.[4]

---

[3] DICKIE J. Costs and benefits of running a computerized personnel system, in PAGE T. (ed), *Computers in Personnel: Towards the Personnel Office of the Future*, IMS/IPM, 1983, pp 38–48

[4] IVE T. *op cit*

In addition to providing an improved information service to the rest of the organization, a range of further applications of immediate benefit to the personnel function itself are made available by computerization and these will be considered in the next chapter.

Other benefits

Computerization also provides a number of other potential benefits in comparison with the shortcomings of manual systems noted earlier. These include:

Improved accuracy Whilst computerized systems still depend upon the accuracy of the data being fed in, the opportunities for feeding in inaccurate data should be reduced. First, computerized systems do not depend upon constantly copying data from one record to another as in manual systems. Apart from data which will be updated at regular intervals, such as pay, personnel records contain a considerable amount of data which is static or relatively static, eg personal data such as name, date of birth, date of entering employment, even job title, grade and address in many cases. Once these data have been fed in accurately, they will remain accurate until any item is changed. Secondly, good software systems should be capable of validating or 'editing' data and detecting errors in a number of ways, including the following:

- criterion checks for particular fields (such as error warning if a salary is above or below a certain minimum or maximum, or if age exceeds 65)
- link checks (eg for example that salary is incompatible with grade, date of joining is at least 16 years after date of birth, etc).

Reduction in fragmentation and duplication All data about individual employees can be stored together in a single system which will be able to provide a complete picture of each employee. Other user departments outside the personnel function can be provided with an on-line link into the database from remote terminals, programmed with passwords to enable them to access and update only those parts of the database which are necessary for their specific needs.

To sum up the benefits of computerized personnel records in comparison to manual systems, computers are able to offer opportunities for:

- reducing or containing rising administrative costs
- increasing the efficiency of the administrative operations of the personnel department
- providing a more comprehensive human resource information service to the rest of the organization, quickly and flexibly
- enhancing the influence of the personnel function on key decisions.

3 Potential uses and applications of computers in personnel work

All the data held about employees which are held in a manual records system are potentially capable of being transferred to computer files. The applications of the computer may be summarized as follows:

- a computerized record system
- a generator of personnel information
- an aid to personnel administration
- an aid to various specialist techniques of personnel management

This chapter sets out a list of potential applications of computers to personnel management. The list is intended to be illustrative rather than exhaustive. A number of personnel systems will not be capable of providing all the applications listed here, but equally there are likely to be other applications available which have not been listed.

Personnel record keeping

The keeping of employee records is the fundamental function of computers in relation to personnel work. Each employee record is stored in the database and may be called up for viewing on the VDU screen, provided that the system is on-line, or, more appropriately, a series of screens which will be called up to view the complete record. The screen consists of a standard format, akin to a record card, on to which data may be entered, updated or deleted by means of a keyboard. Some personnel packages come with screens already formatted and in some cases these formats can be changed to meet user requirements either by the users themselves or by the software supplier who can tailor screens to the user's specifications. Most personnel packages are also referred to as menu driven. This means that screens contain listings of the fields of data held in the system and these can be located by moving the cursor on the screen to the desired field. Hard copies of the personnel records may be obtained by instructing the computer to print and in the case of batch-processed systems, records will be kept in the form of computer printouts or on microfiche copies of printouts.

A good personnel system should enable the personnel department to store all the information currently held manually about employees on a computer, if so desired. Such information should normally include:

- personal details
- current and past jobs and salaries, with dates of changes
- education and training history
- employee benefits
- appraisal details
- disciplinary records
- holidays and absence details
- medical details
- other relevant details.

Some systems also incorporate details of the organization as well as the individuals working in it, such as:

- division
- location
- department
- establishment numbers by job title
- job descriptions
- grades
- other relevant details.

Finally, most systems should enable the user to keep historical files of past employees, useful for identifying trends and making projections, for example, when developing human resource plans.

Report generation

A good system should enable the user to manipulate any of the items stored on the database as required by means of software referred to as a 'report generator'. Most systems come with a certain pre-packaged facility for producing the more common standard reports, such as analyses or listings of employees by job, grade, department, etc which ought to be redefinable by the user. For indefinable enquiries, the user will be required to learn, with the aid of initial training and a manual of operating instructions, how to instruct the software to sort out and list the data required. This generally involves English-type instructions following a strict, logical sequence of precoded numbers, letters or symbols. *Ad hoc* enquiry facilities provide personnel departments with new opportunities to indentify employees with certain characteristics in a way which would have been extremely time-consuming (and might not even have been attempted) with manual record systems. For example, a good report generator should be able to sort out an enquiry such as: 'List all employees, aged 30 to 50, earning under £15,000, qualified to degree level and fluent in French and German'.

Another useful facility provided by some systems as part of the report generation process is known as a diary facility. This facility can be called up to cover a certain period of time, eg the forthcoming month, and will produce a list of action required by the personnel department on the basis of information held in the database. Thus, it will list such information as staff due for a salary review or appraisal in the coming period, forthcoming retirements, forthcoming long service awards and so on. This is particularly useful where salary reviews are based on personal anniversary dates.

Word processing and integrated letter writing

The computing power available to personnel departments may also be used to run word processing equipment with the addition of the appropriate software. This provides the facility to integrate the word processing system with the computerized personnel system and a number of benefits immediately flow from this.

The value of stand-alone word processing (ie not linked to the personnel database) has been recognized for some time by personnel departments. It has been possible to store in the word processor a range of standard contracts of employment or a variety of standard clauses which can be selected and merged together in order to reduce

the amount of typing necessary when producing employment contracts for new employees. In addition, a wide range of texts can be
stored to meet other purposes, eg salary reveiw letters, invitations to
interview and various other standardized responses to the results of
interviews.

Linking word processing to the computerized personnel system
provides further opportunities to automate standard administrative
procedures and provide integrated letter-writing facilities. For
example, systems can be established which automatically produce a
salary review letter, appropriate to the grade or occupation of the
employee, as soon as salary review details have been fed into the computer. In the case of an employee being transferred abroad, the
instruction to the computer to change the location of the employee
will produce a letter setting out the terms and conditions of employment appropriate to that location.

Recruitment

The facility for integrated letter-writing, described above, can be
developed further to create a computerized recruitment administration system. When organizations are engaged in recruitment campaigns, these can generate a considerable administrative task: receiving applications, responding, sending invitations to one or more interview, making the selection and informing successful and unsuccessful
applicants. Apart from the volume of letter-writing involved, the
system has to be supported by a manually prepared log of the progress
of applicants through the system.

Under a computerized procedure, the basic details of applicants can
be put onto the computer and their progress through the recruitment
procedure can be fed into the computer in the same way. In addition,
a range of standard reply letters are stored and these can be automatically produced for sending to the applicant as appropriate. For example, where the initial screening of candidates' application forms
results in a large number of rejections, the computer can be instructed
to record this and letters for unsuccessful applicants will be produced
automatically. The progress of the other candidates through the
recruitment procedure will be recorded on computer and the appropriate letters can be activated as necessary. Such systems can provide
management with progress reports on the filling of vacancies in their
departments and also enable the personnel function to let applicants
know immediately, on request, how their application is proceeding

through the system. If required, the data gathered may also be stored for the purposes of future analysis, for example, of sources of recruitment.

As will be evident from the Directory in Part II of this publication, not all personnel packages provide a recruitment administration facility and of those that do, it usually comes as an additional module to the standard package at extra cost.

Wage and salary planning

The planning of wage and salary increases is a time-consuming process by manual means, but is easily handled by a good computer system. Prior to entering pay negotiations or granting pay increases, a variety of options exist for increasing one or other element of the pay packet or granting one group of employees X%, another Y%, another Z% and so on. The variety of possible permutations is infinite. In addition, further calculations are necessary where increases in basic rates will bring about automatic increases to other elements in the pay packet (overtime, sick pay, holiday pay, possibly shift pay, etc.) linked to basic rates. Stories abound, many of them apocryphal, about calculations being made 'on the back of an envelope' prior to or during pay negotiations. With a computer, it is a relatively easy matter to feed into it what are sometimes termed 'what if?' questions to calculate the cost of an increase in any of the elements of a pay package, improvements in benefits or reductions in basic hours of work. A good system should be able to calculate the costs of any range of options under consideration and to list the consequent effect of these options on the pay of each individual without altering the salary records of individuals until instructed to do so. Good systems should also be able to provide an automatic global update to the salary records held once changes to the pay packet have been determined, eg 'add 5% to the salary of all employees' or 'add X% to one group of employees and Y% to another', and where there is an integrated letter-writing facility, automatically produce letters to employees informing them of their new pay rates.

Absence, sickness and SSP

The keeping of absence and sickness statistics is a relatively straightforward matter to computerize although they may require a considerable amount of storage space. Data on the dates of each absence, the length of the absence and the reasons for it can be stored against the record of each employee. For reporting purposes, this information can be summarized periodically according to the variables stored on the database, eg by department, job, age, etc, using a report generator, as well as providing listings of the absence records of individuals. Absence data can also be readily summarized for calculating the cost where improvements to the sick pay scheme are being considered.

Whilst the computerization of Statutory Sick Pay (SSP) administration has been built into the computerized payroll system of many organizations, there are software packages available which enable the administration of SSP on the computerized personnel system, usually available as an optional, additional module at extra cost.

Human resource planning

Computers can assist the process of human resource planning in a number of ways. First, they greatly enhance the scope of the personnel department to analyse the structure and composition of the current labour force which in itself will provide useful information for human resource planning purposes. Secondly, they facilitate the use of more sophisticated manpower modelling (usually by means of specially designed packages) to make projections and ask questions which simulate future patterns of the organization's human resource system.

Much of the information and analysis which is possible in any standard computerized personnel system will be of value to human resource planning. Thus, the system will be readily able to identify employees with particular qualifications or experience to meet internal vacancies or promotion opportunities. It should be able to produce age analyses by occupation which will highlight potential problems of replacement as a result of forthcoming retirements. It may also calculate patterns of labour turnover by occupation and length of service, useful for predicting wastage patterns and so on.

In addition to an improvement in information about the present workforce and historical trends, a number of modelling packages are available into which data from the personnel system can be fed for making projections and simulations. A number of these packages are available from the Institute of Manpower Studies covering the following kinds of applications:

- models for predicting wastage patterns

- models for simulating manpower flows into, within and out of the organization
- models for simulating career structures against a range of assumptions about organizational growth or contraction.

Further information about these packages is set out in the Directory in Part II of this guide.

Personnel costing and control

Some computerized personnel systems build in a facility to provide line management with regular reports on staff numbers and costs against budget or target, including information on absence, turnover and overtime levels and costs, which may be indicative of inefficiencies in the utilization of human resources.

Job analysis

A number of specialist packages are available which facilitate the process of job analysis. The approaches of computer packages to job analysis vary. Some systems are based upon information supplied by job holders or managers on questionnaires, the results of which may be fed into the computer for analysis and comparison. One system available, referred to as an 'expert system', comes with a wide range of questions and prompts to the user, facilitating a detailed analysis of jobs, via a VDU screen, directly into the system. These packages are described in more detail in the Directory in Part II.

Job evaluation

Computers have also been used by personnel departments as an aid to job evaluation. During the evaluation process, the scores attached to each of the factors in a job can be recorded on the computer. Where the evaluation process involves a large number of jobs, it may be useful for the evaluators to call up at later stages information on the scores already attached. For example, if there is debate on whether a particular job should score, say 4 or 5 for physical effort, it is possible to call for a listing of all jobs previously rated at 4 or 5 for this factor as a basis of comparison. Computers can also be used to simulate the effects of altering the weightings attached to different factors and it is possible to see the effect on the rank order of jobs by inputting different weightings to the factors. In these ways, computers can be used to improve the consistency with which jobs are evaluated, but do not replace the judgemental processes involved. The Directory in Part II describes a software package which provides this facility.

Pay negotiations

It will be evident from what has already been said about the use of the computer for wage and salary planning or modelling purposes that it can also be of considerable assistance during negotiations. With a comprehensive database containing all the elements of the reward package and their costs, it is possible for managment to cost the union claim and to cost various packages of counter proposals which management may wish to put forward. The computer, therefore, helps management negotiators to calculate immediately the costs of a range of options whilst ensuring that any settlement reached remains within the previously-agreed budget or target.

Training and development

A computerized personnel records system provides organizations with speedier and readier access to information about the skills, education, qualifications, appraisal ratings, career history, etc of employees. This will assist in identifying suitable candidates for promotion and indicate what further training or development may be necessary.

Some systems also maintain succession plans for key jobs which show a list of people who could succeed the present job holder and another list showing those people who could succeed to the job in two to five years' time.

Additionally, some systems have been developed to assist training administration. For example, the personnel database stores records about the courses attended and their costs which can be summarized in a variety of report formats. More sophisticated systems can be developed to monitor follow-up training identified as a result of appraisals and the system itself can be used to manage training course bookings and associated correspondence.

Most good packages enable basic training records to be held. Through the use of additional modules or the purchase of separate, specialist applications software, more extensive analyses can be carried out for training and development purposes. Further information about these is contained in the Directory in Part II of this guide.

Staff scheduling, rostering and shift modelling

Some organizations are faced with widely-fluctuating demands for their services which result in highly complex work patterns into which the available labour must be scheduled on a planned and economic basis. Such situations occur particularly in retailing and banking where customer demand fluctuates according to the time of the day and day of the week, and also in passenger transport where demand can vary by the hour of the day, day of the week, season of the year and so on.

Producing rosters manually which meet these fluctuating requirements, but at the same time utilize labour as effectively as possible, has been complex and not always highly effective. Specialized programmes have therefore been developed which enable management, by feeding into the computer data on the staff available and the work demands of various tasks, to create a roster which meets the requirements in as cost effective a way as possible.

Whilst a number of organizations have developed their own tailor-made software for staff scheduling purposes, few ready-made packages are available; an example of one is contained in the Directory in Part II.

Graphics

As the final item in this review of uses and applications of computers in personnel work, it is also worth noting the capability of computers to produce output in the form of graphs and charts well as in tabular form, given the appropriate software and peripherals. A variety of chart forms is possible, including conventional graphs, horizontal and vertical bar charts, frequency distributions, histograms, tulip diagrams and pie charts.

4 The options available for computerizing personnel systems

This chapter should be read in close conjunction with Chapter 5 which provides a step-by-step approach to implementation. Clearly the options available in principle to personnel functions may in practice be limited by a number of factors, including organizational or budgetary constraints, the expertise available in the organization and the specific needs of the personnel function before any final decision is taken. In principle, all the options for computerizing discussed in Chapter 1 are available to personnel departments.

Hardware

The choices for in-house hardware for a computerized personnel system are:

- mainframe computers
- minicomputers
- microcomputers.

Mainframes
Most medium to large organizations possess a mainframe computer in-house, providing centralized computing services for the organization in the fields of accounting and payroll administration. Whilst a separate mainframe computer can rarely, if ever, be dedicated solely to the purpose of processing personnel records or even personnel and payroll, there are often strong arguments put forward for the personnel function to share the existing mainframe with other internal users.

This argument is particularly forceful if there is spare capacity on the computer, since increasing its capacity to do new work will spread the costs of a heavy item of capital expenditure. In addition, the firm will already have in place computer staff to support the development and implementation of in-house systems. The availability of specialist internal support staff may be an additional attraction to the personnel function which may have little knowledge of computing amongst its staff. Indeed, as the survey of current practice will indicate in Chapter 6, the use of the company's mainframe computer has proved the single most widely-used means of computerizing personnel records in recent years, although it is declining in favour of smaller departmentally-based, mini and microcomputers.

The main advantages of using in-house mainframe computers may be summarized as follows:

- *high power* Mainframes are the most powerful type of computer capable of storing high volumes of data, carrying out a complex variety of computations and are fully capable of providing a comprehensive personnel information system with a wide variety of applications.

- *multi-level password facilities* Most good personnel systems enable the head of the user department, for example the senior personnel executive, to specify which items of data can be accessed or amended by which members of staff. The system then automatically controls who gains access by a system of passwords used by staff when accessing the system. The highly sophisticated software available for mainframes means that an almost infinite variety of password controls can be used to control access to the mainframe database.

- *reliability* Mainframes are less prone to hardware problems in comparison with minis and micros and can be programmed to provide better back-up facilities to preserve data when systems failures occur, providing greater security against the accidental loss of data.

- *in-house DP support* The use of the in-house mainframe will normally mean that a full hardware and software back-up and support service will be available internally.

Their main disadvantages include the following:

- *problems with batch-processing* Mainframe computers were originally conceived as batch-processing machines, although on-line facilities have become increasingly common. If batch-processing facilities only are available in-house, this presents a number of drawbacks for the personnel department. In particular, personnel work may be given a low priority in relation to what may be seen as more urgent tasks such as processing invoices or payroll. As a result, the personnel department will lack up-to-date printouts of information in the system because of these time lags and may never be absolutely sure that decisions are being made or information provided on the basis of accurate information. Batch-processing will reduce the direct control of the personnel department over the processing of its data. It should be noted, however, that some personnel departments using a mainframe personnel system satisfactorily operate on a basis of mixed on-line and batch-processing, using on-line facilities for handling immediate enquiries and batch-processing for producing standard or routine reports.
- *problems with on-line facilities* The other alternative, on-line interactive facilities, is a considerable improvement on batch-processing, since it allows the personnel department to interrogate its database directly. Nevertheless, there may also be drawbacks with on-line facilities with which potential personnel users should be familiar. First, high usage of the in-house mainframe may mean that the personnel department's access to it may be restricted to certain times of the day as a matter of policy. Secondly even where there are no such formal restrictions, gaining on-line access may be difficult or very slow when the computer is processing high volumes of data. Personnel departments considering the mainframe option will need to enquire further about these potential difficulties to ensure that their effectiveness in responding promptly to requests for information is not to be impaired.
- *restricted software options* Although the issue of software options are to be considred in the Directory in Part II of this guide, it is worth making reference to this here as it is highly pertinent when considering the mainframe option for personnel systems. Selecting a mainframe tends to limit the options available to buy a

ready-made software package, since the number of mainframe packages available specifically for personnel applications are few. This leaves the option of custom-made software, produced either in-house or externally by a software house, which, as will be described later, can be costly, time-consuming and may not always produce satisfactory results.

- *Security problems* Personnel data often contain private and confidential information about individuals which, under manual systems, would be kept under lock and key in the personnel department. Using a mainframe inevitably means that this data is passing out of the personnel function, increasing the number of people who are potentially able to gain access to the data, eg computer staff. The importance of data security, whilst always significant for DP departments, is more so now in the light of data users' liability for unauthorized disclosure of data under the Data Protection Act (see page 57). Whilst the problems of security of data can be diminished by means of properly-considered procedures and multi-level password access (detailed above), it should be noted that the problem of security is less with minis and micros which are housed within the personnel department.
- *user-friendliness* This is a term used by computer people to denote how readily a computer may be used by non-computer specialists. Whilst modern computer systems are usually more user-friendly in the sense that users will be able to communicate with them using English-type instructions, this may not be the case with older mainframe systems which may require the acquisition of a considerable amount of knowledge for the inexperienced, non-computer specialist to use the facility.

Minicomputers
Whilst the acquisition of a mainframe computer dedicated to the processing of personnel information can rarely, if ever, be justified, minicomputers are less expensive and have been purchased increasingly in recent years for the sole use of the personnel function. As a guide, microcomputer hardware can cost between £30,000 – £80,000. The main advantage of the minicomputer over sharing the in-house mainframe is that the personnel function has total control over its computing facilities. Where sharing is involved, control over information passes out of the hands of the personnel function. In situations where only batch-processing facilities are available, the processing of

data for the personnel function may be given lower priority than, say, payroll or invoicing, resulting in the problems of time lags in receiving up-to-date information, as referred to earlier. Even where on-line facilities are available to the mainframe, gaining access may be delayed where the computer has been overloaded processing high volumes of data for a range of user departments. For larger companies storing arid processing large volumes of data about employees, the selection of hardware frequently involves a straight choice between sharing the mainframe or purchasing a dedicated minicomputer for the use of the personnel department.

Some of the main features of minicomputers in relation to other forms of hardware include the following:

- minicomputers, in principle, do not require additional investment in the provision of an air-conditioned environment, as is the case with mainframes. In practice, however, the heat generated by them usually means that they are best located in a separate room with air extracting fans available. Environment is not an issue with microcomputers.
- minicomputers, unlike mainframe computers, do not require any prior knowledge of computing in order to operate them, nor does the organization necessarily need in-house computer expertise to be available. Nevertheless, in the event of breakdown, it is useful to have computer expertise available in-house and it should also be noted that the training required to operate minicomputers is more extensive than that required for micros.
- where the minicomputer has been acquired for the sole use of the personnel department, this enables full departmental control over how and when data are processed and the data themselves may be kept more securely within the personnel department. This avoids the problems of access time, time lags and the risks of disclosing confidential data referred to earlier.
- minicomputers are less expensive than mainframes, but more expensive than micros. For many personnel departments, minicomputers may still be too costly an option and in any case provide greater storage and processing capacity than would be needed by the personnel departments of many smaller to medium sized organizations.
- minicomputers operate on powerful software providing extensive facilities for storing and analysing data for reporting purposes.

- as described in the Directory in Part II of this guide, a wide range of software packages are available for minicomputers, although it should be noted that much of this software has been written to run on particular models of minicomputer.
- minicomputer systems are capable of supporting large numbers of terminals accessing the database at any one time. As indicated in the Directory in Part II, the number of terminals which can be supported varies from system to system, but ranges from around two dozen to over a hundred or more in the case of some systems.
- minicomputer software tends to be straightforward for the non-specialist to use and normally involves the use of 'English-like' instructions which can be learned relatively easily.

Microcomputers

The growing sophistication of microcomputers means that they are increasingly being considered as a viable option for computerizing personnel information. As well as having the benefit, as with the minicomputer, that control over data processing is entirely within the control of the personnel department, they are also comparatively cheap. Minicomputers which, as discussed in the previous section, could cost around in the range of £30,000 – £80,000 for the hardware and associated software remain too expensive for many personnel departments. A complete microcomputer system which could cost £5,000 – £15,000 therefore makes this option particularly attractive. In addition there is a growing range of packaged software available from which to choose, enabling the personnel department to implement a system relatively quickly. In terms of performance, the development of hard disk technology has increased the storage capacity of microcomputers, enabling them to hold the records of a few thousand employees. The number of employees about whom information can be stored on a microcomputer varies from system to system and according to the amount of data a user wishes to store about each. Typically, microcomputers can be used to store data on up to about 5,000 employees using a 10 megabyte hard disk.

Some of the main features of a microcomputer system include the following:
- they can be installed at a lower cost than mainframe or minicomputer systems: not only are hardware costs lower but so generally are the prices of software packages.
- a wide range of packaged software for microcomputer-based

personnel systems is now available on the market in addition to a range of general business software packages for word processing and spreadsheet work on personal computers.

- microcomputers started life as single-user systems supporting on a single terminal for inputting, amending and outputting data. A number of personnel systems on the market are still single-user systems, but an increasing number of packages provide multi-user facilities, supporting up to between half a dozen and a dozen terminals. It should be noted that the addition of further terminals to certain microcomputer systems may reduce response times when accessing the database.
- generally less knowledge and expertise is required to operate microcomputers and use their enquiry facilities than for mainframes and minis.
- microcomputers, being highly portable, do not require any special environmental conditions for their operation.

Bureaux

For a number of years a range of commercial computer bureaux has been able to offer clients access to specially developed personnel systems based on their own powerful mainframe computers. The essence of the bureau approach is that all the personnel data which a client wishes to computerize is stored in the bureau's computer and access to it is obtained either by batch-processing or real time processing. Bureaux can provide batch-processing services in which the client supplies data, usually in the form of handwritten forms, for in-putting into the bureau's computer. The bureau will then provide the client with batches of printouts according to the arrangements agreed and may also be able to provide further special or one-off analyses at the client's request. More commonly bureaux provide a time-sharing service enabling clients to interrogate their own data stored on the bureau's computer via an on-line telephone link at a terminal in the client's office. Apart from providing the hardware and the software, bureaux will usually also provide training in the techniques of inter-rogating the database, together with a user's manual and associated advisory and consultancy services. Clearly the availability of an on-line link to the bureau is an important consideration for personnel functions since they are likely to need access to their complete record system at any time in order to respond to *ad hoc* enquiries.

The way in which bureaux charge for their services is variable and sometimes complex. They may charge for the amount of disk space taken up by the data stored by the client, the number of CPU seconds taken to process the data and, in the case of on-line links, the amount of computer time used by the client. One difficulty for personnel departments contemplating using a bureau service is estimating in advance the amount of CPU seconds which will be used and the likely costs that will be incurred.

Bureaux enable personnel functions to dispense with complex decisions about hardware and software, but also have certain advantages and disadvantages as a solution to the establishment of a computerized personnel information system.

The main advantages of using bureaux include:

- *Speed of implementation* Using a commercial bureau with a well tried and tested system can enable the personel function to establish a computerized personnel system relatively quickly, particularly in relation to the option of developing a system in-house from scratch.
- *Low capital costs* Using a bureau avoids the need to acquire hardware in-house which can represent an expensive item of capital expenditure, especially when taking into account maintenance and depreciation costs, staff overheads and so on. This benefit is clearly less if in-house hardware already exists and spare capacity is available.
- *Personnel control* Bureaux provide personnel departments with considerable control over their own computing facilities, although the issue of data security is important since data are being processed outside the personnel department itself.
- *Provision of bureau* The use of a bureau external to the organization obviates the need for in-house DP expertise, although as in the case of buying minis and micros, the availability of either internal or independent specialist advice will be helpful when selecting a bureau. However, bureaux do provide their own specialist expertise which is useful when setting up systems and for advising on how to make the most of the system's capabilities.
- *System enhancement* As part of their service, bureaux regularly enhance their systems and offer new services which provide users

with additional facilities without incurring the costs of developing new applications in-house.

The major disadvantage of the bureau is the high operating cost which is likely to be much greater than the cost of in-house facilities once these are up and running. Where the user needs an on-line facility which is regularly in use during the working day, high costs can be incurred because of the large amount of computer time used. Costs can be saved by opting for a batch-processing system or for a mix of batch-processing and on-line facilities, but this will suffer from the drawbacks of such systems which were discussed earlier.

5 A step-by-step approach to establishing a computerized personnel system

This chapter is concerned with a systematic approach to establishing a system, in particular identifying needs and acquiring the software and hardware to meet those needs. The order in which the following activities are carried out is flexible. It may be that not all organizations would wish to follow this sequence; some, for example, might wish to do much more detailed work on identifying needs and designing system specifications before making presentations or putting forward budget proposals to top management.

Familiarization with the field of computers

Before embarking on a computer project, the personnel specialist should aim to become as familiar with the field as possible before putting forward any formal proposals in-house or approaching software houses for details of packages. It is particularly easy to be impressed by suppliers' presentations when the prospective computer user knows little about the subject and fails to ask the right questions. Beyond this, it is also essential that potential users know what they want any system to do before embarking on the selection or development of appropriate software and associated hardware.

It is suggested that the following programme will provide a useful starter for familiarizing oneself with the subject:

Reading Reading provides a starting point for getting to grips with the subject and a recommended reading list of the key publications in the field of computers in personnel is set out at the end of Part I of this guide. However, reading cannot be a substitute for 'first hand' experience and it is important to augment this with opportunities to use a computer terminal.

Courses, conferences and exhibitions Courses in this field are run by the Institute of Personnel Management and the Institute of Manpower Studies who should be contacted for further information. Particularly useful is the annual conference and exhibition on computers in personnel run jointly by these two organizations in London, usually in June or July. The two-day conference enables participants to select from a range of options sessions which are appropriate to their needs and depth of understanding of the subject. The associated exhibition provides a major venue for suppliers to show what they have available.

Advisory bodies The main bodies providing independent advice in this field are again the Institute of Personnel Management and the Institute of Manpower Studies. They will be able to advise on their evaluation of the packaged software available and also advise on or provide the services of independent consultants. Potential users with little experience in the field of computing and with little or no expertise available elsewhere in their organization may well find it useful and cost effective to acquire the assistance of an independent consultant. The national advisory body in the field of computing generally is the National Computing Centre who may also be able to provide some general assistance in this field.

Other companies At this stage also it will be extremely useful to use whatever contacts are available to visit the personnel departments of other companies who have already installed computerized systems. Talking to personnel computer users will provide more insights into the pros and cons of various approaches than talking to suppliers of systems. A number of suppliers of software packages list in their advertising brochures the names of organizations using their systems, but it is better to visit companies known to you or your colleagues for a really independent assessment. A number of approaches to the computerization of personnel records have been considered - mainframe, mini, micro and bureau - and it would be helpful when arranging visits to speak to users who have opted for one or other of these various approaches, if appropriate. A range of issues, set out later in the chapter, can form the basis of questions which may be asked, but it will be particularly useful to ask what the system can and cannot do and whether it has lived up to the expectations of it prior to installation.

In-house expertise   Where there is a data processing (DP) department in the organization, it is obvious that it should also be used as a source of information, albeit on an informal basis at this stage since only initial enquiries are being made rather than firm development plans. Pressures should also be resisted for the DP department to carry out the investigation on behalf of the personnel function or to offer to put up proposals for an in-house system utilizing the exisiting mainframe. Whilst DP assistance when attending exhibitions or visiting companies will be useful, it is important that control of the initiative remains within the personnel department and no options are at this stage closed off.

Securing top management commitment and seeking budget guidelines

After completing the familiarization stage, the personnel specialist should have a fair idea of the options available, their costs and some of the advantages and disadvantages of the various approaches. Additionally a view should have been reached as to whether computerization will be relevant to the needs of the personnel department in question. If it is decided that the issue is worth more detailed investigation, it would be appropriate at this stage to discuss the matter further with those who will eventually approve the project (eg managing director, personnel director, etc). No firm proposals are being put forward as yet, but it will be helpful to seek support and guidance on the following issues:

- carrying out a further feasibility study
- establishing a project team or steering group to oversee the exercise
- obtaining some guidance on the budget likely to be available for implementing a computerized personnel system (which may in turn immediately limit the options which will be available)
- obtaining support in principle for the establishment of a computerized personnel system.

This initial approach should be accompanied by the presentation of a report to support the need for a computerized system and should include:

- indications of the expected benefits, possibly in terms of longer term cash savings, if these are thought likely, but particularly in terms of improvements in management information (see also Chapter 2 for further guidance on the potential benefits of computerization)
- indications of the likely costs of adopting different approaches, ie mainframe, mini, micro or bureau, and estimates of the time and cost of the further feasibility study
- any indications of initial preference, and why
- requests for additional resources needed to carry out further investigations (eg in-house personnel on a project team, temporary assistance in the form of a secondment or external support such as a consultant)
- some indication of the expected time scale of the feasibility exercise.

On the basis of past experience, it is particularly important at this stage that the following mistakes are not made:

- do not be persuaded to hand over the exercise entirely to the DP department on the grounds that they are the experts. Agree to joint participation in a project team with personnel taking the lead, but do not be misled into believing that DP specialists alone will provide a solution which meets your needs.
- do not be over ambitious if your personnel department has no previous experience of computing. 'Keep it simple' is a useful motto: aim initially for a computerized system which will meet all the basic needs of the personnel department. Bear in mind what you may wish to do in the future so as to ensure that any system adopted will be sufficiently flexible to meet future needs.
- do not make promises about the potential benefits of computer systems which in the event may not be fulfilled. Particularly pertinent here are assurances about cost savings through reductions in clerical or administrative staff. Experience has shown that such savings are the exception rather than the rule. The real benefits are likely to be qualitative rather than quantitative in nature.

Establishing a project team

At this stage it is probable that certain parameters to the projects may have been defined, particularly in relation to expenditure. Ideally, parameters should not be defined until system specifications have been drawn up, but in practice many organizations will impose guidelines on expenditure at this stage on the basis of the information on costs already presented. When embarking on the project, therefore, there is likely to be some indication of the potential scale of the task and this in turn will influence the nature of the project team's responsibilities, its make-up and its resources in terms of people and time made available to it. If a major project is envisaged involving substantial expenditure on a comprehensive information system for a large organization, possibly integrating payroll and personnel and pensions, the project team may need to be established to work full time on the task. Members of the team are likely to include personnel, data processing and finance staff, with a senior member of the personnel department in the chair. If, on the other hand, the budget provided, the scale of the project or the organization itself is smaller, with the likely outcome being a microcomputer package, the project may be managed quite adequately by a member of staff from the personnel department with the assistance of an internal data processing specialist or external specialist consultant.

Whatever the scale of the project and the staff resources available to it, the main tasks of the project team will be to:

- carry out an analysis of information needs
- establish the specifications or requirements of a computerized system
- evaluate the options and costs of the software and associated hardware to meet these requirements
- put forward a range of options or a preferred option for approval by top management
- oversee the selection and installation of a system once approval to proceed has been obtained.

Carrying out a needs analysis

A comprehensive analysis of the information needs of the

personnel department is the essential starting phase before moving towards the selection of any system to meet the needs identified. Personnel departments which buy packaged systems without giving careful attention to what the system will be required to do will almost certainly be disappointed with the results. The main issues for the personnel department and the project team to investigate are as follows:

- *What information is currently held and what should be computerized?* Depending on the size and scope of the system envisaged, there may be a need to economize on computer storage space by not computerizing some of the data items held. Key issues to consider include items of data which are rarely used or are never included in reports or analyses produced. For example, personal data about spouses or children may be kept for pension or life assurance purposes, but are rarely referred to. It may be that such data need not be computerized, but could be kept in manual files for reference purposes.

- *What reports and analyses are currently produced?* It will also be important to list what reports are currently produced, eg establishment returns, labour turnover analyses, salary review sheets, sickness and absence returns, to consider whether they are necessary and how they will be affected by computerization. With manual systems, some analyses may have been carried out on a regular basis in case particular questions might be asked. With computerization, it may be necessary to obtain the facility to produce these reports only if asked for them, but not to produce them on a regular basis. It is worth considering also how computerization could enhance the quality of existing reports. For example, more precise analyses of labour turnover by grade, occupation or department may have been too time-consuming to carry out manually, but may be readily carried out by the computer.

- *What reports and analyses might be produced?* This question lies at the very heart of computerizing the personnel record system and is likely to be a major justification for it. It is important that the personnel function does not merely computerize what is currently done, but carries out a full reappraisal of what is done and what might be done. What kinds of personnel information are sought by management, either regularly or on an *ad hoc* basis, which personnel either cannot provide, because carrying out the task manually is too time-consuming and resources are

41

lacking, or take a long time and large resources to supply? This question is concerned fundamentally with the effectiveness of the personnel function as an information provider and requires careful attention. One source of information on this will be the staff of the personnel department itself who will know the difficulties involved in meeting current requests for information and the kinds of requests that are sometimes made. Another obvious source of input is line managers. It is worth setting up an interview programme with line managers and other staff functions to identify what further information or reports and analyses could be usefully provided to meet their needs or alternatively to devise some form of self-completed questionnaire for circulation to relevant users of personnel information. Finally, it is important to consider what further information or analyses would be useful for the personnel function internally, for example analyses of the effectiveness of different recruitment sources or media.

- *What current procedures are followed by members of the personnel function and how will these be affected by computerization?* A number of current procedures may become redundant as a result of computerization and thought needs to be given as to how tasks will be restructured. In addition, new tasks may be added since more information can be produced and again the ways in which this will be handled needs consideration.

- *How much historical data will be computerized?* The keeping of historical data about current and past employees is important for analysing trends and making projections, but again it will be making further calls on the storage space available. Questions to consider include how much historical data should be computerized, which items of data are most relevant for analysis purposes and how far back should computerized historical records go? It may be that historical data going back five years will provide sufficient information on trends and a short profile of the employees concerned, with the dates on which various job changes occurred, will be sufficient for the computerized record, with full details being stored manually as a back-up.

At the end of the needs analysis process, personnel departments should be able to specify in detail:

- the items or fields of data which will be computerized

- the reports which they wish to generate on a regular basis
- the nature of *ad hoc* enquiries which they wish a computerized facility to handle as necessary
- the tasks of the personnel function which will be affected by computerization (for a list of some of the potential applications of computers to personnel work, see Chapter 3).

Designing system specifications

Whilst determining information needs is a task primarily driven by the personnel function in consultation with managers of other functions, designing system specifications is concerned with the more technical elements of the system's performance in which DP specialists will take a leading role. Whilst it is beyond the scope of this book to examine this topic in detail, some of the issues typically considered include the following:

On-line or batch-processing Some of the issues associated with this were considered in Chapters 2 and 4. It is essential, when setting out system specifications, to decide which of these two options will be necessary to meet the requirements set out or whether some combination of the two may be possible. For example, regular or routine reports could be produced on a batch basis, but facilities to respond to *ad hoc* enquiries requiring a swift response would necessitate on-line or interactive facilities.

Screen layouts and report formats The personnel department should specify how data should be grouped and set out on screens and precisely how standard reports should be laid out.

Number of users A basic decision will need to be made on whether the system required will involve one terminal or more and, if a multi-user system is required, how many terminals will be needed. Ideally, there should be one terminal for each member of staff regularly accessing the database but in practice a ratio of one terminal to two staff is more common.

Edit requirement Reference was made in Chapter 2 to the various ways in which data can be edited automatically or validated to ensure a higher level of accuracy when inputting it into the system. A range of possibilities should be considered, including automatic validation of salary input against grade, job title against department or location,

43

date of birth against date of commencing employment, etc.

Interface specifications   Where the proposed system will be required to interface with other existing installations, what technical specifications will be required in order to allow this? For example, what technical specifications are required of a mini or micro to be located within the personnel function to enable it to interface with the existing in-house mainframe or indeed other existing minis or micros?

Privacy and confidentiality   What built-in facilities should the system have to ensure that those accessing data will only be able to do so on a predetermined basis? This will require an analysis of who will be using the system and what information they will be entitled to access and amend. The system must then be capable of understanding a range of passwords used by operators to ensure that each only gains access to the data which they are entitled to see and entitled to alter.

Input/output media   What input media, eg screens and terminals, are required and how many? If, for example, multi-user facilities are required, with a number of operators updating the database at any one time, this must be included in the specification. What output media, eg printers, are required, how many and what quality?

Ease of use   How easily do we expect the system to be used by non-technical staff? Do we expect to carry out substantial and lengthy training to instruct operators or do we need a system capable of handling English-type instructions requiring a few days training?

Audit trails   A number of systems have built-in features for logging automatically who is accessing the system and what amendments have been made. For the purposes of data privacy and security, an 'audit trail' feature may be required by organizations.

Having identified information needs and established the technical requirements of a system, the next stage is to consider the software options for implementing the system. The main options are:

- to evaluate the ready-made packages available
- to evaluate bureaux services
- to evaluate the development of software in-house.

Evaluating ready-made packages

With the requirements of the proposed system carefully specified, an

44

obvious step is to consider whether they can be met by an existing software package. This has a number of advantages. First, it will save on the costs and time involved in developing in-house and secondly, it should enable a system to be implemented more quickly. A potential difficulty is finding a ready-made package which matches the requirements specified.

At this stage, the project team may wish to reactivate some of the initiatives undertaken during the preliminary 'familiarization' stage. Now equipped with more detailed specifications of requirements, it may be worth attending exhibitions or renewing contacts with other companies to look again at the systems available and what they are capable of doing. Alternatively, or in addition, it may be felt that the time is right to approach a number of suppliers of personnel packages, further details of which are provided in the Directory in Part II of this guide. Below is set out a checklist of points to consider when selecting and evaluating suppliers of software packages once detailed specifications have been determined.[5]

Evaluating the status and reputation of the supplier

- how long has the supplier been involved in the field of personnel software and what is its reputation? Obviously the prospective purchaser will want to deal with a firm committed to computer systems in the personnel field so that a longer term, on-going relationship can be established.

- have other users been contacted for information about particular suppliers or have other organizations such as the Institute of Personnel Management and the Institute of Manpower Studies carried out supplier evaluation? Have visits been made to user organizations to talk about various suppliers, both in relation to the technical performance of packages and the general level of support and back-up service provided to users?

- what professional personnel expertise does the supplier have in

---

[5] See also the following which have been used to construct this checklist: WALKER A J, How to evaluate a prepackaged personnel system, *Personnel*, May/June 1979, pp 31–40; HIRSCH W, Choosing a personnel computer system: 20 questions for survival in the DP jungle, *Manpower Studies*, No 4, Spring 1982, pp 3–4; BRYANT-MOLE M and HIRSCH W, *Database Packages for Microcomputers Reviewed: Computers in Manpower Management*, IMS report No 62, Brighton, Institute of Manpower Studies, 1983

addition to DP specialists? This will prove useful when developing longer term relationships by enabling the personnel user to talk to someone who fully understands his problems. It may also indicate some commitment on the part of the supplier to develop or enhance the system on the basis of stated user requirements or new developments in the personnel field.

Evaluating the technical capabilities of the package

- *Database* Does the system employ the use of a database or database management system (DBMS) enabling any of the elements of data held to be combined for the purposes of analysis? Moreover, has the database or DBMS been developed for general business applications or specifically for personnel applications? A number of the packages on the market are general database packages which in practice may not provide the linkage between all the fields of personnel data which may be required for the purposes of analysis or *ad hoc* enquiry.

- *Hardware* Because of the variety of operating systems in use (see Chapter 1) what hardware is compatible with the software on offer? In practice, this may be of specific concern only where hardware has been purchased already or is already available in-house, or compatibility with other in-house hardware is a major consideration.

- *Flexibility of data structure* Can the fields of data already contained in the package be altered or customized to meet the client's individual needs? Whilst the personnel data held by different organizations will tend to be broadly similar, some organizations will want to keep data which others do not and vice versa. Does the structure include 'free fields' (ie fields without a predetermined title or description) within which the user can add categories of data which are intended to be kept? Can the data structure be altered subsequently by the user, ie can new fields be added or existing ones deleted, without calling in professional expertise? Will the system hold all the items of data which a personnel department wishes to store?

- *Validation* Can data be validated, or automatically checked, as they are entered? What validation checks are part of the package, how sophisticated are they and how readily can they be improved upon? Can validation checks be specified by the user or determined once the system has been installed?

- *Data analysis* What sorting and analysis is the system capable of carrying out and how long does this take? Before going to see a demonstration, the needs analysis should have identified the analyses and *ad hoc* enquiries which the personnel function wishes to carry out. Particular points in relation to the varying capabilities of systems to analyse data include the following:

  i   Counting records   Most systems enable the user to list people, eg by grade, but some cannot count the number in each grade

  ii Number of variables   Some systems may limit the number of variables which may be analysed at one time (eg list the people in grade X and above, who are female, aged 35 to 45, and are fluent in French and German). How many variables can the system handle? Ask for a demonstration.

  iii Analysis of historical data   The amount of historical analysis may be limited on certain systems, which may not be able to respond to such enquiries as: 'How many people moved from Grade A to Grade B between date X and date Y?' or 'How many people who were in Grade A on date X left the organization before a certain date?' An associated problem with some systems is that they do not 'understand dates'. According to one expert, Wendy Hirsch, this is a critical area of evaluation and she concludes that "if a system can handle these enquiries, it will handle most things".[6]

  The capability of the system to analyse data as required is a critical part of the evaluation process and should be given close attention when viewing demonstrations. Other points to note relate to the difficulty in setting up the system to respond to random enquiries and response times. How much training will the non-specialist user require to make these enquiries? How long does the system take to respond? When considering reponse times, it is also worth noting that these may slow down when the system is loaded with large amounts of data. It is therefore worth asking suppliers about the number of 'dummy' employee records loaded on to the system for demonstration purposes, which can be verified by seeing the names listed and totalled.

- *Report generation* What kinds of standard listings or reports can be produced and, in the case of random enquiries, how many

---

[6] HIRSCH, W, *op cit*, p 4

variables can be handled for the purposes of cross-tabulation? Can the layout and content of reports be varied to suit the needs of the individual organization? How complex are the procedures for setting up standard reports and, more particularly, *ad hoc* reports? Does the system produce reports using codes only, eg for departments or jobs, or does it have the facility to produce the English equivalent for each code which will make the report more readily intelligible to the user?

● *Security and privacy*   What facilities does the system provide to determine different levels of access to the system (eg by the use of passwords)? How many different levels of password access are available and can these be determined by the user? Does the system incorporate an 'audit trail' logging who has accessed the system and the amendments made?

Evaluating costs and supplierssupport services

● Is the cost of the software and, if appropriate, associated hardware (including peripherals) clearly stated by the supplier?
● Is it clear what is included in this price and what 'hidden extras' there are? For example:

i   What are the charges for customizing the package to meet a user's requirements or for additional, optional modules which are offered over and above the basic package?

ii   Are training courses for users included in the basic package price or charged as extras and, if so, at what rate? What training is being offered? Is it sufficient or will additional training need to be paid for? Is there an instruction manual?

iii What maintenance services are provided? Are these included or extra and, if so, what do they cost? Does maintenance include automatic upgrades to the system?

iv   Is there a 'hot-line' telephone service to advise users?

v   Are delivery charges included in the basic price or do they cost extra and, if so, how much?

vi   Is the product being enhanced? If so, how? When investing in software and possibly also new hardware, it is essential that investment is being made in an ongoing product.

vii Does the supplier run a users' group which enables users to exchange experiences on the way they are using the system and supply feedback and suggestions to the supplier?

When evaluating suppliers, there may be some who are rejected immediately because of fundamental shortcomings in the package in relation to identified needs or basic incompatibilities in respect of hardware. Clearly it is worth establishing some minimum fallback requirements before engaging in detailed evaluation so that time is not wasted.

Detailed evaluation should involve all the members of the project team who, as well as investigating the peformance of the system and the supplier's back-up support in detail, may also follow up any reference given by the supplier. Clearly selecting a supplier requires a wide range of factors to be taken into account and it may be that no supplier comes near matching the specifications required, in which case this option will be inevitably closed off.

Evaluating bureaux services

Some of the main issues to consider when selecting a bureau include the following:

Analysis of the status and reputation of the bureau
i   How long has it been in the field?
ii   What are the views of others, personnel and non-personnel, about its services?
iii Is it offering a system specially developed to meet the needs of the personnel user? Is it providing on-line or batch- processing service or a combination of the two?
iv Does it employ personnel professionals as advisers who understand the needs of personnel users?

Technical analysis of bureau services
The evaluation of the services of each bureau is similar to the evaluation of packaged software which was considered above. In particular, the project team will have clearly identified information needs and specified a number of additional, technical parameters which need to be taken into account.

Analysis of costs
It will be necessary to carry out an evaluation of the way in which the

costs of bureau services are charged (eg amount of data stored, CPU time etc) and the costs of training or other support services in relation to the data processing needs of the personnel function.

In-house development

If neither bureaux services nor ready-made packages are able to meet specified requirements, and it has been decided not to contract out the writing of the software to an independent software house, the remaining alternative is usually to consider in-house development. In the past, most computerized personnel systems have tended to be developed in-house, utilizing capacity on the in-house mainframe, but this approach is probably becoming less predominant with the appearance in recent years of minis and micros, together with fairly flexible ready-made packages. Nevertheless, many organizations feel that neither these nor bureaux services are sufficiently flexible to meet their needs and opt for producing their own custom-made software.

It should be recognized from the outset, however, that developing a personnel system is a major undertaking, in which substantial time and resources will need to be invested and considerable time will elapse before it is implemented. Although the project team will have carried out a lot of useful preliminary work by establishing information needs and specifying systems design parameters, particularly close co-operation between personnel and DP staff through the programme development, testing and implementation phases will now be necessary. The following is a checklist of issues to consider before embarking on the in-house route:

i   How good are the working relationships between DP and personnel? It is vital that personnel remain in control of the project and do not contract out of their responsibilities by handing over the entire task to DP.

ii   Is the system likely to be complex and break new ground technically? If so, does the organization have the expert resources available and is it prepared to allocate these scarce resources to the project, bearing in mind that well qualified DP staff are traditionally in short supply?

iii   To what extent does top management give priority to the project? Traditionally, projects to computerize personnel systems attract lower priority in organizations in comparison with other applications, resulting in delays and overrun schedules on personnel systems projects.

iv   Have DP made realistic estimates of time scales, resources and costs to complete the project and do they fully understand the system requirements in a field which is generally considered to be complex to computerize in comparison with, for example, more standardized accounting procedures?

For more information on the development of in-house systems, the reader is referred to the publication, *Developing a Computerized Personnel System: The Management and Buyer's Guide* by David Burns-Windsor, published by IPM Publications.

Implementing the system

No matter how much hard work has gone into the selection or development of a system, careful attention needs to be paid to the final phase of implementation to ensure that the project is completed smoothly and effectively. The areas requiring particular attention are as follows:

Training   A range of training must be considered to ensure that:
- the staff responsible for the substantial task of entering data into the system are trained in the procedures to be followed
- the staff of the personnel department are trained in all the relevant aspects of the system's operation, encompassing data input, retrieval, amendment, etc, through the prepackaged routines for obtaining standard reports, to the more complex routines involving the use of high level language for responding to *ad hoc* enquiries and complex data search and analysis
- other managers are aware of the system and, where appropriate, the procedures for accessing it.

Data input   The initial task of loading data into the system from manual records is substantial and ideally should be organized to take place at a time when the personnel function is not engaged in one or other of its major annual activities, eg annual pay negotiations or salary reviews, appraisals or recruitment campaigns. On the basis of the information provided in the operating manual, data input staff should be trained in:

- coding data from manual records
- dealing with information gaps in manual records
- following precise instructions for inputting data, eg upper or lower case letters, standard abbreviations and other instructions to ensure consistency of data input
- interpreting and acting upon data error messages.

Personnel departments may consider having temporary staff to carry out this task.

Trial run   Although trial runs are not always possible with ready-made packages, an increasing number of software houses do make systems available for a trial period in the potential user's organization. The records pertaining to one department or smaller location can be loaded up and tested before the system finally 'goes live' to ensure that any remaining problems can be solved.

Parallel running and full implementation   Whether or not a trial run has been possible, there will inevitably be a period in which the new computer system is being thoroughly tested, while at the same time the existing manual records system is being run in parallel. Once the computerized system has been thoroughly tested, the use of all those parts of the manual system which have become redundant as a result of computerization can be discontinued.

6 Recent trends in computerized personnel systems

In order to provide an overview of recent trends, this chapter sets out the results of a number of surveys which have been conducted into the ways in which computers are being developed and applied in personnel departments in the UK[7]. The information has been drawn from the findings of four surveys, conducted between 1982 and 1985, to provide a picture of the trends for users and potential users in personnel departments.

Extent of coverage of personnel systems
The rapid rate of growth in the application of computers to personnel management is indicated in the table on page 54. Survey results indicate that between 1982 and 1985 the number of respondents stating that they had a computerized personnel system rose from 40 to 73 per cent, an increase of 83 per cent in the organizations with a system during this four year period.

---

[7] RICHARDS-CARPENTER C, Filling the information gaps, in *Computers in Personnel*, IPM/IMS, 1982, pp 159–163; CIP: The state of the art and beyond, in *Computers in Personnel: Towards the Personnel Office of the Future*, IPM/IMS, 1983, pp 9–17; TORRINGTON T and HALL L, Few signs of a computer revolution, unpublished paper, Department of Management Services, UMIST, 1984; RICHARDS-CARPENTER C, The 1985 'Computers in personnel' survey results, *Personnel Management*, September 1985, pp 49–50

Year	% of respondents with a computerized personnel system
1982	40%
1983	59%
1984	68%
1985	73%

The 1984 survey also revealed that almost two-thirds of the personnel departments not yet using a computer planned to do so during the following two to three years.

Age of personnel systems
The pace at which computerization is being adopted by personnel functions is indicated in the 1983 survey by an analysis of the age of the systems in use and how this changed between 1982 and 1983.

Age of personnel system	% of responses	
	1982	1983
Less than 2 years	32	54
2 - 5 years	30	23
6 - 10 years	27	16
More than 10 years	11	7

Over half the systems in use in 1983 (54 per cent) had been in use for less than two years, compared with about one-third (32 per cent) one year before, reflecting the fast pace of implementation in the personnel field.

Types of hardware used
The table below indicates some of the main trends in the type of hardware used:

Types of hardware	% of responses		
	1982	1983	1985
Mainframe	76	65	55
Mini	5	11	13
Micro	4	9	24
Word Processor	5	6	4
Bureau	10	9	4

NB 1984 survey results not used because they are not directly comparable

The main trends are a decline in the use of mainframes, probably reflecting the discontinuation of older batch systems and the growth in the use of smaller machines, in particular minis and micros. The growth in the use of microcomputers was particularly marked during this period. The small proportion of respondents using word processors continued to decline during the period. The use of bureaux services fell by more than half, probably reflecting a trend towards in-house hardware, in particular minis and micros.

Records held on personnel systems

The 1984 survey asked respondents about the categories of personnel records stored on computer. The percentage of respondents holding different categories of information is indicated in the table below:

Type of record	Percentage of respondents holding these records on computer %
Payment administration	55
Employee records	45
Absence	30
Fringe benefits	25
Training	24
Recruitment/selection	20
Redundancy/dismissal	13
Appraisal	13
Job evaluation	13
Management development	11
Health, safety, welfare	7
Discipline/grievance	6
Employee relations	3

The authors of the survey conclude that the current application of computers to personnel work focuses mostly on record keeping and routine analysis and reporting. Comparatively few systems incorporate 'modelling' or 'what if?' enquiry facilities and even fewer incorporate integrated letter-writing facilities.

Most useful applications of computers to personnel work

The 1984 survey asked respondents about the most useful applications of the computer in personnel management on the basis of their experience to date. A wide range of benefits were described, the most frequently mentioned in order of priority, being as follows:

i   improved administration of payments systems
ii   improved employee record administration
iii better human resource planning
iv   improved reporting and query facilities
v   improved facilities for analysis and statistical purposes
vi   improved absence recording

Future trends

In order to obtain some impressions of future trends in the applications of computers to personnel work, the 1983 survey asked respondents what new computing facilities were desired in comparison with what was currently available to them. Their responses are set out in the table below.

Applications	% of responses	
	Current (1983)	Desired
Word processing	45	47
Recruitment administration	29	58
Manpower budget administration	27	61
Absence control	25	65
Contract of employment administration	21	60
Job evaluation	18	49
Performance appraisal administration	16	56
Training and development administration	15	69
Manpower numbers forecasting	12	61
Manpower cost forecasting	11	63
Medical/accident administration	11	62
IR negotiations	6	32

The evidence indicates that the applications of computers to personnel work will further develop from being a means of reducing the clerical routines involved in keeping records and producing reports to more integrated administrative systems in which the computer will play a central and indispensible role in the work of the personnel function. In particular, respondents envisaged a widening of computer applications to a range of specialist activities of the personnel function,
including recruitment, selection and associated letters and documentation, job evaluation, training and development, human resource planning, health and safety and industrial relations negotiations.

Postscript: the Data Protection Act

Since 11 November 1985, all data users holding personal data about individuals on computer have been required to register certain particulars of the data held with the Data Protection Registrar, and to comply with the provisions of the Data Protection Act which regulates the way data are gathered, held and disclosed. The data held in computerized personnel systems are subject to the provisions of the Act and must be registered, alongside other categories of personal data held by user departments in organizations.

This section provides a brief overview of the Act. For a full description of the implications of the Act for computerized personnel systems, the reader is referred to the IPM publication *The Data Protection Act - A Guide for Personnel Managers* by Alastair Evans.

Registration

Forms for registering under the Data Protection Act are available in bulk from the office of the Data Protection Registrar, Springfield House, Water Lane, Wilmslow, Cheshire SK9 5AX (tel 0625 535777/ 535711). Smaller quantities of forms are available from Crown Post Offices, where forms and notes of guidance are available in 'registration packs'.

Data users are required to supply the following information on the registration form:

- name and address of the organization
- the purpose or purposes for which data are held

- a listing of the broad categories of data items held
- a description of the sources from which data are or may be gathered
- a description of those to whom data are or may be disclosed
- a listing of countries outside the UK to which data may be transferred
- one or more addresses for the receipt of requests from data subjects for access to the data.

All this information may be supplied using a range of standard descriptions set out in the registration form.

The Data Protection Principles

The Act establishes a set of eight Data Protection Principles with which data users must comply. These are backed up by a combination of criminal and civil sanctions. The Data Protection Principles state that personal data must:

i   be obtained and processed fairly and lawfully
ii   be held only for one or more specified and lawful purposes
iii not be used or disclosed in any manner incompatible with these purposes
iv   be relevant and not excessive for their purpose
v   be accurate and, where necessary, kept up to date
vi   not to be kept for longer than is necessary for their purpose
vii be disclosed on request to the data subject at reasonable intervals
viii be kept secure against unauthorized access, alteration, destruction, disclosure or accidental loss.

Rights of data subjects

The Act provides data subjects (eg employees) with a range of rights in civil law in relation to personal data held about them. These are as follows:

- *rights of access to personal data*   Individuals have the right to ask a data user whether any personal data are held about them and, if so, to receive a written copy of all the personal data held within the meaning of the Act.

- *rights to compensation for inaccurate data*   A data subject who suffers damage as a result of inaccurate factual data being held by the data user has the right to bring an action for compensation against the data user.
- *rights to compensation for loss or destruction or unauthorized disclosure of data*   A data subject who suffers damage as a result of the loss, destruction or unauthorized disclosure of data held by a data user or computer bureau is entitled to bring an action for compensation.
- *rights to apply for rectification or erasure of data*   Whether or not damage has been suffered through the holding of inaccurate data, a data subject has the right to apply to the courts for the rectification or erasure of any data held, including facts and expressions of opinion.

Timetable for implementing the provisions of the Act

The provisions of the Act are being phased in over a period of time and it should be noted that some of the rights of data subjects, referred to above, come into force during 1986 and 1987. A timetable indicating when some of the main provisions of the Act come into force is set out below:

4 July 1984	Data Protection Act passed
4 September 1984	Rights of data subjects to claim compensation for damages arising from the loss or unauthorized disclosure of personal data came into effect
11 November 1985	Registration commenced
10 May 1986	Registration of all existing data users closes and it becomes an offence to hold unregistered data after this date. After this date also the rights of data subjects to claim compensation for damage as a result of inaccurate data come into effect
11 November 1987	The rights of data subjects to request access and receive a written copy of their personal data come into effect

Further reading

BURNS-WINDSOR D, *Developing a Computerized Personnel System: The Management and Buyers' Guide*, London, IPM in association with Brameur Ltd and IMS, 1985

EVANS A, *The Data Protection Act: A Guide for Personnel Managers*, London, IPM, 1984

INCOMES DATA SERVICES, *Computers in Personnel*, April 1983

IVE T, *Personnel Computer Systems*, Maidenhead, McGraw Hill, 1982

IVE T, Computers in Personnel, in Armstrong M, ed, *Personnel and Training Yearbook*, London, Kogan Page, 1985

NORMAN M and EDWARDS T, *Microcomputers in Personnel*, London, IPM, 1984

PAGE T, ed, *Computers in Personnel*, London, IPM/IMS, 1982

PAGE T, ed, *Computers in Personnel: Towards the Personnel Office of the Future*, London, IPM/IMS, 1983

PAGE T, ed, *Computers in Personnel: Making Manpower Profitable*, London, IPM/IMS, 1984

PAGE T, ed, *Computers in Personnel: Today's Decisions - Tomorrow's Opportunities*, London, IPM/IMS, 1985

WALKER A J, *HRIS Development: A Project Team Guide to an Effective Personnel Information System*, New York, Van Nostrand Reinhold, 1982

WILLIE E and HAMMOND V, *The Computer in Personnel Work*, London, IPM, 1981

PART II

DIRECTORY OF SUPPLIERS OF COMPUTERIZED PERSONNEL SYSTEMS

Microcomputer systems

Centre-file Ltd
PO Box 177
75 Leman Street
LONDON E1 8EX
Tel: 01-480 3000

Software package
The Personnel Assistant

Number of installations
See the entry for Missing Link Software below

Company profile
Centre-file is part of the National Westminster Bank Group and offers bureaux services, ready-made or software and hardware, as well as turnkey systems.

Hardware
IBM PC

Software
Centre-file market *The Personnel Assistant* software package designed by Missing Link Software (see entry below). The price of the software starts at £5,000 and complete systems can be offered on a turnkey basis from £10,000. The system can also be linked to 'Centre-pay', a bureau payroll service operated by Centre-file.

The Personnel Assistant is capable of producing a wide variety of reports which can be adapted to a company's own particular needs. Typically, reports fall into three basic types:

i   *Listing reports* Listings of information from records, such as skills, qualifications, languages etc, by department and grade, terms and conditions of employment, salary and career history, absence and overtime summary and promotability.

ii *Formatted reports* These may be adapted for use whenever information has to be laid out in a specific format, such as employee profiles.

iii *Matrix analysis reports* The Matrix Analyser allows information to be analysed in several different ways, eg recruitment cost by source and department, average salary increase by grade and length of service, average absence by grade and employment status etc, and *ad hoc* analysis.

Other features include:

● fully integrated word processing

● a user manual on the screen which enables users to press a 'help' button for instructions when there is a difficulty over entering or extracting information

● data entry validation which rejects incorrect entries

● multi-user/network option enabling the use of up to 12 terminals with each operator sharing the memory unit

● five levels of password

● a data dictionary storing commonly used data, such as job descriptions

● a global update, enabling all records to be modified or updated by means of a single instruction

- automatic recalculation of such data as age and length of service

- the ability to cope with HAY-MSL statistics

- ability to transfer data to or from another computer, eg to or from a payroll, using the optional data transfer module.

Comley Computers Ltd
95 Woodbridge Road
Guildford GU1 4PY
Tel: 0483-35557/36987

Software packages
Mandate and *Payper*

Number of installations
Mandate: 33; *Payper:* 20

Company profile
Comley Computers is a microcomputer software company with a number of years experience in supplying computer systems for personnel applications.

Hardware
Both the programs described below will run on any microcomputer which uses the CP/M, MP/M, MS-DOS or XENIX operating systems. Both programs are available for multi-user application.

Software
The costs of the two packages are as follows:

Mandate   Single user £300; multi-user £500

Payper   £1,500

Mandate is a general purpose database intended for a range of different record-keeping applications in the fields of business, industry and leisure. The user designs the screens according to personal requirements in the same way as forms would be designed on paper. Once formatted, information can be entered on to the blank screens.

Mandate's enquiry option enables records to be extracted from the database using selection criteria specified by the user. A report generator enables the user to compile reports using information on the database for all records or a selection of records, sorted if required. A mailing list option enables the user to combine information from the database with standard letters or reports. Mandate is available with a multi-user facility, with record-locking to prevent two people simultaneously changing the same information.

Payper is an integrated payroll/personnel/SSP system with a capacity to handle the payroll and personnel requirements of companies with up to 5,000 employees. It is available for multi-user access to the database with record locking.

Some of the features of *Payper* include the following:

- *payroll*   A flexible payroll facility allowing payments to be calculated in different ways, handling both weekly and monthly paid employees

- *statutory sick pay (SSP)*   The SSP system enables payments to be calculated automatically from the dates of absence and indicates whether an employee qualifies for SSP. A two-month calendar detailing all current absences is maintained for each employee

- *personnel*   Predefined screens hold personnel information on the system and there are also several blank screens which the user may define

- *security*   Access to the system is controlled by a series of passwords

- *accounting*   The system incorporates payroll cost reporting and cost centre allocation

- *electronic fund transfer*   An additional programme *BACSCOPY* (available at £150 for CP/M, MS-DOS and PC-DOS, operating systems only) enables the payment of salaries via BACS (Bankers Automated Clearing Services)

- *reports*   A variety of reports may be produced for management or statutory purposes by company or cost centre

- *enquiries*   The enquiry system allows the user to select and sort employees by any selection criteria. The Report Generator can be used to produce reports of any information held on these employees

- *history records*   History records are automatically generated by the system whenever key items of data are changed and there is no limit on the number of history records which may be kept for each employee

- *special facilities*   In addition to the standard system, a further library of special reports and facilities is available and customized facilities to meet client needs can also be incorporated.

Compel
39 Prospect Street
Caversham
Reading RG4 8JB
Tel: 0734-473992

Software package
Compel Personnel System

Number of installations
About 90

Company profile
Compel was established in 1982 and its computerized personnel package is based upon a widely-used, general purpose database known as 'Delta', developed by a British software house Compsoft plc.

Hardware
Delta is available for a wide range of 8 and 16 bit microcomputers

using the MS-DOS/PC-DOS, CP/M and MP/M operating systems. Such computers include the IBM PC, ACT Apricot, ACT Sirius, DEC Rainbow, Wang, Xerox and others. The ACT Apricot and Sirius range of microcomputers and associated peripherals are supplied by Compel on a turnkey basis.

Software

The Compsoft Delta database package is a single user system and is supplied at a basic price of £495. In addition, Compel supplies other proprietary software packages including:

- Pulsar Multiplan, Lotus Symphony, Pulsar Supercalc 2 and 3 (spread sheet packages for 'what if?' calculations)

- Pulsar Wordstar and Mailmerge, Software Systems Multimate and Pulsar Super Writer (for word processing)

- Praxis Microchart Plus and Super (for graphics)

- communications links to other computers.

System design, implementation and support services are provided at a daily consultancy rate of £350.

In addition to the supply of hardware and software, Compel also provide the following services:

- advice and assistance on the identification of computer needs

- system design

- implementation, including customization to meet client needs

- user support through telephone 'hotlines', further training, software upgrades and periodic meetings of users to exchange ideas.

Some of the features of Delta include the following:

- standard and user defined screens

- multi-level password access

- record sorting numerically, alphabetically, by date or a combination of these

- records search in response to *ad hoc* enquiries using up to eight search criteria simultaneously

- printing of lists and reports in accordance with various parameters

- storing of letters and merging of these with information stored in the records

- transfer of selected information into Wordstar or other user-written software.

Comshare Ltd
10 Grosvenor Gardens
London SW1W ODH
Tel: 01-730 9991

Software package
Profiles/PC

Number of installations
200 (USA); new package in UK: 10 installed

Company profile
Comshare is a computer software and services company established in the USA almost 20 years ago and has been operating in Britain for the last 15 years. Initially concentrating on providing a computer bureau service, the company now also provides packaged software for micro, mini and mainframe computers. This section is concerned with Comshare's personnel software for the microcomputer; for further information on the company's personnel software for the mini-computer, see the appropriate section below.

Hardware

Comshare's personnel software for the microcomputer is designed to run on the IBM PC with hard disk, IBM PC/XT or AT with a minimum memory of 512K byte running under the PC-DOS operating system. The software may also be run on any 100 per cent IBM PC compatible machine (eg Compaq Plus).

Software

Profiles/PC is available at £4,950, plus an installation and training charge of £1,000 and an annual maintenance charge of £745. For any company with less than 2,000 employees, *Profiles/PC* provides a complete personnel system; for the larger organization the system can be linked to other existing mainframe installations. The system comes as an off-the-shelf package with a predefined database that can be used without modification, but also allows the user to modify or replace menus, field names, add new fields, etc.

Some of the other features of *Profiles/PC* include the following:

- 35 standard reports are included as part of the package

- A Report Writer for producing other non-standard or *ad hoc* reports

- No limitation on the amount of historical data stored

- Three levels of password access

- 'Help' keys providing explanations where data entries are not accepted.

The Comshare maintenance agreement includes a telephone 'hot-line' support and enhancements to the system on an on-going basis.

I-Data plc
Scawthorpe Hall
Great North Road
Doncaster DN5 7UN
Tel: 0302-786677

Software package
R-Staff

Number of installations
New package

Company profile
The company has been in existence for two and a half years, is an authorized remarketer of IBM Series 1 minicomputers and is a systems house for the PICK operating system.

Hardware
R-Staff has been developed to run under the REVELATION operating system and is compatible with most microcomputers running on PC-DOS and MS-DOS, including the IBM PC range, ACT Apricot, DEC Rainbow, Sperry PC, Texas Instruments Professional Computer, Wang Professional and others. REVELATION is also capable of supporting a multi-user network. A 10 Mbyte disk is recommended for up to 5,000 employees and the hardware costs of a typical system, consisting of IBM PC/XT, 10 Mbyte disk and printer, would cost in the region of £6,000.

Software
The price of the *R-Staff* software package commences at £1,600. The package consists of two main files: the Employee File and the Post File. The Employee File contains personal information, salary data, career history and absence information. The Post File covers jobs and grades.

Other features of the system include the following:

• password control governing updating/amendment of records

• standard reports

- *ad hoc* and 'what if?' enquiry facilities

- batch updating of salaries and holidays

- leaver details listing

- benefits listing

- pension and bonus scheme breakdown.

Intereurope Software Design
3 The Courtyard
Wokingham RG11 2AY
Tel: 0734 787365

Software package
PERPAC

Number of installations
New package

Company profile
The company is the software division of Intereurope Technical Services Ltd and a member of the Intereurope Technology Services plc group.

Hardware
PERPAC is designed to run on microcomputers running the CP/M, MP/M, MS-DOS, Turbo-DOS or PC-DOS operating systems. It requires RAM memory of 48K or more free user area (exclusive of operating system requirements) and a mass storage capability of at least two floppy disk drives and each with at least 320 Kbytes of usable (floppy disk) storage capacity after formatting. Additional drives, disk capacity or hard disks will increase system performance. Hard disks are recommended.

Software

PERPAC costs approximately £855 for single user and approximately £1,600 for multi-user, the precise cost being dependent upon the extent of additional programming. The full procedural language, at an additional cost of £565 for single user and £800 for multi-user, will be required where experienced users wish to modify *PERPAC* themselves.

The package consists of a nucleus of data field file structures which can be tailored and amended to meet users' needs. Standard reports and data entry screens may also be tailored to users' requirements. The package also includes a selective report generator. Alternatively, experienced users can purchase the entire procedural language, as described above, in order to expand or modify the package.

International Computers Ltd (ICL)
Personnel and Payroll Applications Products
Cavendish Road
Stevenage SG1 2DY
Tel: 0438-313361

Software
Personnel 20

Number of installations
100

Company profile
ICL is Europe's leading computer manufacturer and supplies computer systems, software and associated services. It operates in more than 75 countries throughout the world and is the only British owned large scale designer and manufacturer of mainframe computers. ICL is now wholly owned by Standard Telephone and Cables plc.

Hardware
Personnel 20 runs on ICL's DRX software compatible with ICL's DRS 20 System microcomputer hardware. It may be used as a single

or multi-user system or may be linked to ICL's mainframe personnel system (System 29 · see mainframe section below). With the appropriate communications programme, *Personnel 20* may also be interfaced with IBM or IBM compatible hardware.

Software
The starting price of *Personnel 20* is £3,100. The package enables the user to specify the information to be stored, the layout of the screens and the links between them. Typical items of information stored in the system include:

- personal details

- career details

- status details, eg department, job, grade, entitlements

- salary-related details

- establishment details, eg organization structure, posts, cost codes

- absence details.

Other features of the system include:

- validation checks for data entry

- bulk update facility

- multiple level password access

- audit trail/logging of users

- integrated letter-writing (requiring the addition of ICL's DTM text processing package)

- standard reports specified by the user and stored in the system

- *ad hoc* and 'what if?' reporting facilities.

KCS Management Systems
Whitecliff House
852 Brighton Road
Purley CR2 2UY
Tel: 01-660 2444

Software package
Persona

Number of installations
10

Company profile
KCS was formed in 1971 as a software company designing, developing and maintaining systems for accounting, payroll and personnel purposes. The company is part of an international organization with over 250 users of their accounting and payroll systems (K-Paye) worldwide. More recently, the company has developed a specialist personnel system for microcomputers called *Persona*.

Hardware
Persona operates on microcomputers with MS-DOS/PC-DOS operating systems and a complete system running on the Wang PC is supplied on a turnkey basis. The company is also launching an integrated personnel and payroll package, available on the Wang VS minicomputer.

Software
Persona is a single-user system available at £1,750, inclusive of one day on-site support and six days training. Annual maintenance is charged at 12% of sale price and additional on-site support is charged at £250 per day.
    The main features of *Persona* include the following:

- maximum number of files which may be set up range from eight in the basic version to 1,000 in the full system

- screen layouts can be tailored to user requirements

- a range of passwords are used to enable full access, update access or enquiry access only

- standard and *ad hoc* reporting

- integrated letter writing

- facilities to store historical records.

LMR Computer Services
54-70 Moorbridge Road
Maidenhead SL6 8BN
Tel: 0628 37123

Software package
ADPM2 (Adaptive Personnel Management System for micro-computers)

Number of installations
New package in July 1985

Company profile
LMR was established in 1971 to provide a computer bureau service and has since expanded into programme products and turnkey systems in the fields of personnel, payroll, accounting, production and management information systems. LMR became part of UEI plc, a group of high technology companies.

Hardware
ADPM2 is available on any multi-user microcomputer using the UNIX operating system.

Software
ADPM2 is a recently launched software package, based upon LMR's *ADPM* package for minicomputers described in the appropriate section below.
   The system has a number of elements including:

- establishment records, which are the foundation of the system

76

- applicant records, which allow the progress of an applicant to be followed from initial contact through to rejection or job offer

- employee records, covering all personal details, benefits, sickness, absence, training and qualifications

- leavers' and pensioners' details.

A further feature of *ADPM2* is that it can be upgraded when the database has grown in size and demands upon it have increased to a minicomputer application, with the advantage that the software will continue to be familiar to the user.

The costs of the system depend on the size of the micro used; software prices are also lower where turnkey systems are supplied.

The lowest costs of *ADPM2* modules are as follows:

- personnel management: £2,500

- database management (for report generation, *ad hoc* enquiry, etc): £1,000

- payroll: £750

- SSP: £750

- word processing: £650

- spreadsheets: £920.

MSS Services Ltd
31a Chapel Road
Worthing BN11 1EG
Tel: 0903-34755/6

Software package
Personnel and Manpower Management

Number of installations
6

Company profile
MSS management systems, selection and training consultants, have a range of software packages in the fields of manufacturing and accounting and also produce an employee records package.

Hardware
The package runs on the IPB-PC, Apple and Epson QX10 micro-computers or other microcomputers using the CP/M80, CP/M86, PC-DOS, or SOS operating systems.

Software
The price of the package is £400 and enables the recording of employee details, in addition to absence, performance, training, disciplinary data, etc. Other features include:

● 'what if?' enquiry facility

● prompts about forward events such as a change of pay due to age or forthcoming retirement

● facilities to incorporate a word processing package to provide personalized letters, contracts of employment etc.

Mimex Business Systems
40 Triton Square
London NW1 3HG
Tel: 01-387 4599

Software package
Personnel Aid

Number of installations
25

78

Company profile
Mimex is a software house and systems integrator, specializing in software packages and tailor-made turnkey systems for use in the field of personnel management and recruitment.

Hardware
The Mimex *Personnel Aid* software package operates on micro-computers with an MS-DOS operating system (eg IBM PC, ACT Apricot and Sirius) or on Concurrent CP/M or MS-NET for multi-user systems. As computer dealers for ACT Apricot and Sirius, turnkey systems are provided using these computers and associated peripherals.

Software
The *Personnel Aid* software package is available in three versions:

i   a version limited to 23 fields at £495

ii   a 46 field system at £695

iii   a new 255 field system (recently tested at customer sites) at £895.

The 23 and 46 field versions have been installed and running in user organizations for the last two years.
   The main features of *Personnel Aid* are as follows:

- may be tailored to user needs in relation to data entry and retrieval

- designed to work with Wordstar word processing software for standard and personalized letters

- user-defined function keys

- select and search facility on all fields

- sort facility on all fields

- batch updating facility

- file merging facility for correspondence and mailing lists

- user-defined reports.

Microcalc Ltd
55 Lower O'Connell Street
Dublin 1
Eire
Tel: Dublin (0001) 730173/730055/730204

Software package
Your Man

Number of installations
New package

Company profile
Microcalc offers a range of computer services, including off- the-shelf and tailor-made software, hardware, software and hardware maintenance support and computer training.

Hardware
The Microcalc personnel package, known as *Your Man*, can be installed on any microcomputer running on CP/M, MS-DOS or PC-DOS operating systems. Microcalc also supplies and installs Sperry PCs.

Software
The basic software package retails at £850 and produces reports on:

- absenteeism

- holidays

- staff probation

- labour turnover

- past employees

- written warnings

- nominal roll.

The product has been left open-ended to include tailored reports and other enhancements which Microcalc designs to customer specifications.

Missing Link Software
65 Maygrove Road
London NW6 2EG
Tel: 01-625 5111

Software package
The Personnel Assistant

Number of installations
50

Company profile
Missing Link Software was established in 1981 to develop and market specialized software packages and the expertise of the company is centred on the design and development of database management systems, in particular *The Personnel Assistant* software package.

Hardware
The Personnel Assistant may be run on microcomputers using the MS-DOS, PC-DOS and Concurrent CP/M3.1 operating systems. It will therefore run on most top microcomputers including IBM, Wang, HP, DEC, Sirius and Apricot, either as a single terminal or multi-user system. The company will supply hardware as part of a turnkey deal.

Software details
The costings of *The Personnel Assistant* software are as follows:

	No of terminals			
	1	2	3	4
Basic price	£3995	£3995	£3995	£3995
Customizing option	500	500	500	500
Multi-user option	-	2400	3300	4200
Software support - 12 months (including hot-line)	600	960	1095	1230
Delivery/implementation (within 50 miles radius of London)*	200	300	300	300
Training - 2 days on site, 4 trainees per session (within 50 miles radius of London)*	400	400	400	400
TOTAL	£5695	£8555	£9590	£10625

*Delivery, installation and training on sites outside the 50 mile radius from London will be subject to a surcharge based on distance.

Further optional modules
Absentee recording module	£500
Data transfer module, eg interface with mainframe	£400
Link to *Centrepay* payroll available on selected hardware, eg IBM PC	£200

The Personnel Assistant is available as either a single-user or multi-user system, in the latter case allowing simultaneous access to the database by up to 12 operators. Software for the multi-user system costs £2,400 for the first terminal and a further £900 for each terminal thereafter.

Typically, *The Personnel Assistant* would be used to keep the records of an average 2,500 employees using a 10 megabyte hard disk, but more employees than this could be handled. The system is supplied, ready to use, with a set of eight standard screens, ie eight pages of information for each employee, but these may also be customized to suit individual requirements.

The features of *The Personnel Assistant* include the following:

- operator's manual/'help' screen: this may be called up and displayed on the screen itself

- validation checks

- automatic calculation of age, length of service etc each time a record is accessed

- passwords: a five level password system

- data dictionary for storing standard, frequently-used data items

- integrated word processing for standard letters, documents, etc is incorporated as part of the system

- reports, defined by the user

- global update/modification of records

- searching and sorting of information by any field on the database.

Percom Ltd
11 Golders Green Road
London NW11 8DY
Tel: 01-458 4326

Software package
IMP (Integrated Modular Personnel System)

Number of installations
65

Company profile
Established in 1982, Percom is an independent software house concentrating on the development and marketing of personnel management systems for a range of microcomputers.

Hardware
IMP is a single- or multi-user system, available for microcomputers using the MS-DOS, PC-DOS, Concurrent CP/M and Unix operating systems. Turnkey deals are available and current hardware options include the IBM PC/XT and AT, ACT Sirius and HP150.

Software details
Costs of the *IMP* personnel management system are as follows:

	No of terminals				
	1	2	3	4	5
Basic price, including flexi-screens, absence recording and integrated letter writer	£4950	£4950	£4950	£4950	£4950
Multi-user option	-	2000	2000	2950	3900
Total software cost	£4950	£6950	£6950	£7900	£8850

Service costs

Delivery, implementation and training (3 days)	£900
Additional on-site training (per day)	£350
Software maintenance (per annum)	15% of software price
Customization (per day)	£300
Consultancy (per day)	£350

Optional modules

	Bolt-on	Stand-alone
SSP	-	£850
Recruitment	£1250	(price on application)

Career planning	£950	-
Wordstar word processing	£494	-

Other utilities:

Single-user upgrade to multi-user (including two additional terminals)	£3000
4th and 5th terminals (each)	£950
Data transfer utility	(price on application)

The *IMP* package is supplied, ready to use, with a range of predefined screens for capturing core data in addition to a facility known as *flexiscreens*, through which users can customize their own screens to meet their needs. The database is sub-divided into three groups to provide information on:

- employee details

- job and organizational information

- job and employee attributes, eg skills, qualifications, experience, training etc.

Other features of the *IMP* system include the following:

- menu driven, with 'help' screens, prompts and messages

- 40 standard reports and analyses

- *ad hoc* reporting facility

- mass update of common changes to information in the system

- multi-user facility enabling the use of at least eight terminals, depending on the hardware, with record locking and queuing, and 'multi-tasking', to enable more than one operation to be performed simultaneously on the same processor

- four levels of password controls

- audit trail to log transactions

- diary reports to remind users of forthcoming action needed, eg long services award, appraisal, retirement, pay award etc with the facility for these to be defined by the user

Percom also operate a 'fair trial' system enabling a potential buyer to use *IMP* at their place of work for six weeks: further details may be obtained on application to the company.

Quadra Computer Services Ltd
Maltby Trading Estate
Rotherham Road
Maltby S66 8EL
Tel: 0709-815475

Software package
Quadra Personnel Management System

Number of installations
17 (micro and minicomputer versions)

Company profile
Quadra Computer Services is a computer consultancy, software, hardware and service organization operating from South Yorkshire, London and Edinburgh. Standard packages include accounting, payroll, personnel, production and distribution applications. Bespoke software is also prepared to meet specialist needs.

Hardware
The Quadra Personnel Management System has been written to run on micros using the CP/M or UNIX operating systems and an NCR micro is supplied as part of a turnkey arrangement.
NB: The *Quadra* System is also available for NCR I-Series mini-computers: see appropriate section below.

Software

For a description of the *Quadra Personnel Managment System*, see the company's entry in the 'minicomputer' section on page 109.

Radius Ltd
Wykeland House
47 Queen Street
Hull HU1 1UU
Tel: 0482-227181

Software package
Radius Personnel System (micro version)

Number of installations
See Radius entry in minicomputer section on page 111.

Company profile
Radius has been operating as a computer supply and services company since 1976. Originally providing on-line and batch processing facilities on a mainframe computer, Radius expanded into the supply and maintenance of turnkey mini/micro systems in 1981 and is the main supplier of Texas Instruments computers in Europe.

Hardware
The micro version of the *Radius Personnel System* is available for microcomputers using the MS-DOS, CP/M86 and Concurrent CP/M86 operating systems. The package is available on a turnkey basis on the Texas Instruments range of microcomputers. Radius also produces a minicomputer version which is described on page 111.

Software
The cost of the Radius system is £400. The package comes with 12 fixed fields for personnel data and up to 40 further user-defined fields. Reports are achieved by running the 'Selective Personnel Report' which enables the user to select up to 20 different fields for reporting

purposes. Reports may be printed according to a standard format or in a format specified by the user.

Team Computer Services Ltd
Team House
High Street
Syston LE7 8GP
Tel: 0533-601874

Software package
Personnel 20

Number of installations
100

Company profile
The company was originally established in 1969 and has existed in its present form since 1975. It has a close association with ICL and provides a range of ready-made and bespoke software packages covering such fields as payroll, personnel, sales and accounting, as well as bureau services, hardware and turnkey systems.

Hardware
Personnel 20 is ICL's own software package for ICL microcomputers which is available through Team Computer Services (as well as direct from ICL). For further information on hardware, see the ICL entry elsewhere in this section.

Software
The starting price of *Personnel 20* is £3,100. For further information, see the ICL entry elsewhere on page 73.

Team Computers have also been developing their own software package, *Teampersonnel* which is not yet available. Further information about its availability may be obtained direct from the company.

The Wyatt Company (UK) Ltd
Park Gate
21 Tothill Street
London SW1H 9LL
Tel: 01-222 8033

Software package
ABACUS (microcomputer version)

Number of installations
New package

Company profile
The Wyatt Company is an international actuarial, employee benefit and compensation consulting firm operating through offices in Europe, North America and the Far East, providing consulting services in such fields as pensions administration, profit-sharing, salary administration, executive compensation, and financial and insurance company consulting.

Hardware
The *ABACUS* package for microcomputers is designed to run on the IBM PC/XT and AT. The package is also available for minicomputers and as a bureau service (see page 115).

Software
The package has been available as a bureau service and for an in-house PRIME minicomputer (see page 115) and has recently been made available as a microcomputer application. The microcomputer package is aimed at smaller organizations and the price is available on application to the company. For further information about the general characteristics of the *ABACUS* package, see the Wyatt Company entry on page 115.

Minicomputer systems

Barron McCann Ltd
Barron McCann House
Shortmead Street
Biggleswade SG18 OAT
Tel: 0767-316286

Software package
Personnel 25 Plus

Number of installations
12 (plus 30 upgraded from an earlier system)

Company profile
Barron McCann supplies a range of standard software packages for mini and microcomputers, including accounting, stock control, management information and personnel systems, and also develops bespoke programs. The company co-operates closely with ICL, particularly in relation to software and specialist hardware design applications.

Hardware
Personnel 25 Plus is available for the ICL System 25 range of minicomputers, which can be supplied alongside all necessary peripherals as part of a turnkey deal.

Software
Personnel 25 Plus retails at £20,000+. The package had its origins in a package known as *PINICL*, a personnel package developed in 1978 for use on the predecessor of the ICL System 25 (System Ten) and has

been redeveloped during that time, particularly during the last 18 months. The system can be configured to meet the personnel information needs of small, medium and large organizations, ranging from a few hundred up to 50,000 employees.

Features of the system and related complimentary software, include the following:

- user-defined reports, the formats of which can be stored in the system, using up to 16 selection criteria. More complex reports can be produced with System 25's own report writer, *INFORM 25*

- *ad hoc* enquiry and 'what if?' modelling facilities

- multiple level password access determined by the user

- integrated word processing and linkages to other microcomputers, using ICL's 'WORDSKILL 25' and 'PCLINC' software packages

- batch or global update facilities

- networking facilities to enable the system to communicate with either ICL or IBM mainframes via a variety of specialist protocol converters or communications couplers

- absence and SSP recording

- data dictionary facility containing standardized data items determined and amended by the user

- full job logging and audit trail options, including who used which program.

To support implementation and installation, Barron McCann offers three levels of Implementation Advisory Package:

- Package A: Basic Installation: this lasts for two days at the customer's site and is the minimum installation package a customer must take.

- Package B: Initial Implementation: this lasts for five days and covers basic installation, plus some advisory and training time.

- Package C: Full Implementation: this lasts 10 days and provides basic installation, setting up of an initial dictionary, plus advisory and training time.

CMG Information Consultancy Services Ltd
Westway House
320 Ruislip Road East
Greenford UB6 9BW
Tel: 01-578 4563

Software package
CMG-PERS

Number of installations
Two

Company profile
CMG-PERS has been designed and developed by CMG Computer Management Group, one of Europe's leading independent computer services companies.

Hardware
CMG-PERS is written in the PICK-based PRIME Fourth Generation Language and is designed to run on the PRIME 50 series of mini-computers. The system requires a single computer processing unit and will support up to about 26 display/entry units or can operate as a component in a network of distributed processors. In some configurations, it will operate in a normal office environment and without the need for specialist data processing knowledge.

Software
CMG-PERS is available at a single licence fee of £10,000, which includes 10 man days of implementation and customization. The

92

system is presented as a standard package, but with the facility to add or interface with other modules, such as payroll, SSP or recruitment.

Features of the system include the following:

- menu-driven screens, with data validation at the time of entry

- data dictionary holding standardized data

- a set of standard reports, plus the facility of an *ad hoc* report generator to produce other reports defined by the user

- a range of security password levels defined by the user at the time of installation

- a file of security violations maintained by the system.

Coggon Computers Ltd
Snaithing Grange
Snaithing Lane
Sheffield S10 3LF
Tel: 0742-307481

Software package
PERSON

Number of installations
Two

Company profile
Originally established in 1968 to provide bureau services, the company has existed in its present form since 1977 to provide a turnkey solution for organizations requiring in-house computing. Standard and bespoke software is supplied for a range of applications, including payroll, personnel, pensions, accounting, manufacturing and other business applications.

Hardware
PERSON operates on the IBM Series 38 and Hewlett Packard HP3000 minicomputers, both of which can be supplied as part of a turnkey deal.

Software
The price of the software is £10,000, which includes 10 days' training and implementation help. The software is supplied as a standard package which can be customized to meet precise user requirements.

The main features of the system include:

- general table feature-up to 26 tables are available, so that descriptive data which are used frequently can be be defined by code, allowing fast input of information, consistency of description and elimination of misspelling

- standard information held for each employee under 'personal' and 'employment' headings

- standard personal information which includes personal details of employees, such as name, address, age, education, qualifications, etc

- standard employment information includes details of current employment, details of previous employment, absence and sickness history, including SSP

- user defined information allows up to 100 further items of information to be held per employee, definable by the user

- user defined screens which can be set up by the user to display either standard or user defined information in the format required, in addition to the pre-defined screens provided within *PERSON*

- automatic transfer of payroll information (optional) – the Coggon *PAYPLAN* option enables the transfer of data to and from other systems for payroll and SSP purposes

- standard reports which include audit, monthly and quarterly personnel statistics, and full or partial printing of information held on file. The audit report provides a report to the personnel department on who has been amending the personnel database

- blanket changes and 'what if' reporting features are included to facilitate the implementation of salary/wage changes, and to assist the forecasting of the effect of proposed changes

- user defined reports – up to 94 additional reports are available which can be defined as required to meet current and future management requirements

- ease of use – *PERSON* uses keys with plain English labels to aid the use of the system by personnel department staff. A 'help' function key is also provided, which can be accessed at any time during operation and displays a detailed reminder of the facilities available within the current operation.

Co-Cam Computer Services (UK) Ltd
89 Kingsway
London WC2B 6RH
Tel: 01-404 5881

Software package
CHARM (Customized Human Resources Management System)

Number of installations
10

Company profile
Co-Cam is the name given to a software tool developed in 1976 for a range of applications, including payroll, pensions, personnel and accounting. Co-Cam Computer Services is a joint venture company established by two firms of consulting actuaries and the company is

involved in the provision of software, hardware and associated support services.

Hardware
The system will run on any computer in the Hewlett-Packard HP3000 series range, although other hardware options are expected to be added in the future. The starting price of the hardware is approximately £20,000. The hardware and software are supplied under a single contract. The package is also available on a bureau basis, using Co-Cam's computer based in London (see page 131).

Software
The *CHARM* personnel system is geared particularly to the needs of large organizations and is supplied in the form of a number of independent modules, covering:

- a basic personnel record system

- a sophisticated report generator

- graphics

- manpower planning

- organization and running of training programmes

- recruitment

- letter-writing and word processing

- down-loading to microcomputers.

The precise cost of the system varies according to which modules the user chooses and the extent to which they are customized to meet an organization's needs. The starting price for a system is £5,000.

The personnel package is one of three integrated packages: the others cover payroll and pensions. Each may be purchased separately or as a complete, integrated system. The personnel system can interface with most other packages available on the HP3000 range of computers.

The main features of the package include:

- multi-level security facility to protect against unauthorized access, use or modification of the database. This can be tailored to suit the needs of the user organization and can be subsequently altered by the user

- standard reports and *ad hoc* enquiry facilities which allow any information in the database to be listed, summarized or combined according to the selection criteria of the user

- 'what if?' analysis and reporting

- integrated word processing

- audit trail provisions and transactions logging

- range of data validation facilities.

Comshare Ltd
10 Grosvenor Gardens
London SW1W ODH
Tel: 01-730 9991

Software package
Profiles/3000

Number of installations
250 + (worldwide); 10 in UK

Company profile
See page 69

Hardware
Profiles/3000 is designed to run on any model in the Hewlett Packard HP3000 minicomputer series, including the low-end Series 37, running the MPE operating system.

Software
Profiles/3000 was introduced in 1982 and is built around a standard Hewlett Packard *IMAGE* database so that it is compatible with all standard HP utilities. The database is configurable to the customer's specification and captures details of both employee and applicant records.

The costs of the software package are as follows:

Profiles/3000

software licence	£15,000
training and installation (2 weeks)	£ 2,000
maintenance (annual renewable)	£ 1,800 or 12% of software cost for multiple copies

Discounts are available on multiple copy purchases.

The main features of the system include:

- menu driven system

- database which allows information to be stored on employees and applicants, including personal details, education, salary, skills, job history, etc

- a range of standard reports on a variety of topics such as employee profiles, skill searches, job history, labour turnover, salary distributions, organization charts and mailing lists

- *ad hoc* reporting facilities

- absence recording

- recruitment administration

- salary modelling

- industrial injury monitoring

- multiple level password access

- audit trail logging access to the system.

Crestbond Ltd
12 Canbury Passage
Richmond Road
Kingston-upon-Thames KT2 5BG
Tel: 01-549 8933

Software package
Crestbond Personnel Information System

Number of installations
Five

Company profile
Crestbond was founded in 1971 and specializes in mini and micro-computer software, bureau services, data preparation and turnkey systems.

Hardware
The Crestbond system runs on the IBM System 34 and 36 and the Wang VS range of minicomputers. IBM or Wang computers could be supplied as part of a turnkey deal.

Software
The price of the package is £3,000 with an annual licence fee of £500. The information held by the system is contained in eight screens for each employee, each screen containing the following information:

- personal details

- next of kin details

- employment details

- education details

- current job details

- job/salary history

- benefits

- training record.

A range of standard reports are available from the system and a report generator enables *ad hoc* enquiry and reporting according to criteria selected by the user.

Cybertek Computing Ltd
Cybertek House
Heath Hurst Road
London NW3 2RX
Tel: 01-435 4425

Software package
Cybertek CPS (Computerized Personnel System)

Number of installations
10

Company profile
Cybertek specializes in developing fourth generation software products for Data General computer users. The company was founded in 1977 and its customers include a range of businesses and public authorities in the UK, North America, Europe and Australasia.

100

Hardware

Cybertek CPS operates on the entire range of Data General mini-computers runnning the AOS and AOS/VS operating systems and the system is generally used by medium to larger organizations. Hardware costs are in the region of £40,000 and the system is capable of supporting up to 32 terminals.

Software

The basic software price is £25,000. At its most basic level, the CPS system holds standard personnel information such as personal details, qualifications, overtime worked, career history, salary, training courses attended, absenteeism etc. However, all systems can be specially tailored to meet each user's specific requirements.

In addition to CPS, other related products in the Cybertek software range include:

- *CYBERQUERY* a powerful enquiry package and report writer which enables users to ask virtually any questions about data contained in the computer files

- *CYBERWRITER* also available as a fully integrated option for producing personalized letters, with information being taken from any number of files

- *CYBERSCREEN* creates screens for menus, inputs and browsing.

Other features of the system include:

- data transfer to and from other personnel-related applications, such as payroll and pensions

- flexible screen manipulation, allowing any screen to be modified as desired and new screens to be created if users wish to store additional information

- multi-level password security control, defined by the user

- standard reports and *ad hoc* enquiries, drawing information from any combination of files.

Foster Wheeler Energy Ltd
Foster Wheeler House
Station Road
Reading RG1 1LX
Tel: 0734-585211

Software package
PERSEUS

Number of installations
Six

Company profile
PERSEUS is the Foster Wheeler Personnel Computer System, developed and used by the company's personnel department, and has been marketed by the Company to other user organizations for the past four years.

Hardware
PERSEUS runs on the Hewlett Packard HP 3000 range of mini-computers. The starting price for the hardware is £16,000 and the system is capable of supporting a very large number of terminals.

Software
Software costs depend on the number of additional modules purchased. The basic personnel records package would cost approximately £9,000, but a fully comprehensive system with all the options (as described below) could cost £40,000. The package offered includes software, full training and expert assistance with implementation.

The main features of the system include:

- over 100 standard reports

- other standard and *ad hoc* reports can be produced by the user by means of the powerful report generator

- integrated letter writing, with letters being generated automatically when records are updated

- a recruitment administration facility which maintains detailed records of applicants and vacancies and produces letters automatically, including contracts of employment

- facility to produce skills inventories, using up to 16 screens, each with 40 items of expertise as specified by the user

- absence analysis and SSP calculation

- global update facility

- reports for manpower planning purposes, including age profiles, service, wastage, career performance, progression and potential

- multi-level password system enabling access to be restricted to individual data item level

- facility to pass specified information to and from other systems, such as payroll and pensions.

LMR Computer Services
54-70 Moorbridge Road
Maidenhead SL6 8BN
Tel: 0628-37123

Software package
ADPM (Adaptive Personnel Management System for minicomputers)

Number of installations
13

Company profile
See page 76

Hardware
ADPM is designed to run on *PRIME* minicomputers for which

turnkey facilities are available. The package is also available as ADPM2 on a microcomputer with the multi-user UNIX operating system and as a bureau service (see pages 76 and 133).

Software
The price of the basic personnel records package is £12,000. Further customization can be undertaken by the client or, at extra cost, by LMR. The remainder of the ADPM package consists of a range of optional additional modules which may be purchased at extra cost. These are as follows:

- recruitment module which aids the administration of recruitment procedures covering invitations to interview, references, results of interviews through to rejection or commencement of employment

- employment module which holds the personal details of employees and career histories

- pensions module used for administering pension records and the calculation and payment of pensions

- establishment module which keeps details of posts which can be linked to current postholders in the employee records system

- leavers module which stores the records of leavers and provides analyses on leaving patterns.

ADPM can be further modified and extended by the use of the following additional, related software packages:

- *ADEPT* for word processing and integrated letter writing

- *ADIN* for screen format generation

- *ADOUT* for report generation.

ADPM is one of a suite of three systems, the others being the *ADPAY* payroll system (which also includes an optional SSP module) and *ADSKIL*, a job analysis package for use in manpower planning, training and development and job evaluation. *ADPM*, *ADPAY* and *ADSKIL* are available as fully integrated or stand alone systems. ADSKIL is described further on page 138.

Microdata Information Systems Ltd
Maylands House
Maylands Avenue
Hemel Hempstead HP2 4RL
Tel: 0442-61266

Software package
Microdata Personnel System

Number of installations
134

Company profile
Microdata, part of McDonnell Douglas, is Britain's third largest supplier of large minicomputer and networked computer systems. The software for the system is written by Isis Computer Services, an independent British software house established nine years ago and based in Bristol.

Hardware
The *Microdata Personnel System* runs on the Microdata M6000 minicomputer, the Microdata 8000 local area network and the Microdata M9000 supermini for very large systems.

Software
The cost of the software depends on the number of modules and the extent of customization. The software is available on a rental basis and the basic package starts at about £400 a month. Special applications packages are also available for personnel administration and other applications in the police, local government and the health authorities.

The Microdata package sets out the basic system elements and

105

thereafter there is considerable latitude to adapt the system to the user's requirements. The system contains three interrelated files:

i personnel files which hold personal data about employees

ii establishment files which hold data about posts, departments, organizational units, etc and budgetted and actual numbers of employees

iii job description files containing details of each job description, grade, and salary ranges.

Additional modules include:

• facility to link the personnel system to payroll and pensions systems

• sickness and absence recording

• integrated word processing and standard letter writting.

Osprey Computer Services Ltd
Budds Lane Trading Estate
Romsey SO5 OHR
Tel: 0794-517979

Software package
Osprey Personnel Management System

Number of installations
Seven

Company profile
Osprey were established in 1973 and produce a range of ready-made packages and custom-built software for IBM computers covering a

wide range of business applications, including personnel, finance, banking, transport and others.

Hardware
The *Osprey Personnel Management System* is available for the IBM minicomputers System 34 and System 36 and, as an appointed IBM agent, Osprey can supply the hardware as part of a turnkey deal.

Software
The package consists of a basic personnel records system with up to 50 optional additional modules to enhance the system. The cost of the basic package is £2,100 and the price of additional modules varies between £60 for a simple report to £700 for complex analytical packages. The purchase of all modules would add about £11,000 to the basic price. Modules can also be added gradually when the facilities are required. The standard packages may also be tailored to client needs at an additional charge. The Osprey package has been on the market for about five years and is capable of supporting up to 36 local and 64 remote users.

The main features of the system include:

- recording of full, personal details, including career history, skills, qualifications, training details, holiday monitoring, etc

- calculation of bonuses and profit share

- personalized letters

- recruitment administration from initial enquiry through to commencement of employment or rejection

- standard reports, *ad hoc* enquiries and salary modelling

- multi-level password security

- multiple tasking and multiple access, enabling different tasks to be performed by many users at the same time

- audit trail reports on who is accessing the system.

PM Associates Ltd
Century House
57-59 Frith Road
Croydon CRO 1TB
Tel: 01-688 6047

Software package
PM Associates Personnel System

Number of installations
New system

Company profile
PM Associates was formed in 1980 to provide real time bureau facilities to companies without their own computers. The company has expanded to provide additional services, including software development and the provision of turnkey solutions in the fields of accounting, insurance, pensions and personnel.

Hardware
The package runs on PRIME minicomputers or any other machine which will support the Pick (fourth generation) software. Hardware prices start at £8,000 for a four-terminal system and can be supplied on a turnkey basis.

Software
The price of the software is dependent on the size of the organization and ranges from £7,000 to £15,000.
   At the time of writing, the product had not yet been launched and only a limited amount of information was available about this system. The basic system provides for nine screens of information for each employee covering the following:

- employee personal details

- next of kin details

- education and special interests

- employment history

- salary history

- employee benefits

- company property

- training courses attended

- attendance records.

A recruitment module is also available consisting of four sections:

- registering the recruitment

- registering each application

- registering each applicant's background/skills

- interview/test tracking.

Quadra Computer Services Ltd
Maltby Trading Estate
Rotherham Road
Maltby S66 8EL
Tel: 0709-815475

Software package
Quadra Personnel Management System

Number of installations
17 (micro and minicomputer versions)

Company profile
See page 86.

Hardware
The Quadra system has been written to run on NCR I-Series minicomputers which can be supplied as part of a turnkey arrange-

ment. It is also available as a microcomputer system: see page 86.

Software
The system comes in the form of a core module and a number of optional additional modules:

- *core information* provides personal and employment details, eg holiday, sickness and absence monitoring; cost – £1,200

- *additional information* provides six additional user-named files for information of a descriptive or historical nature; cost – £300

- *ad hoc report* generator allows information to be retrieved as specified by the user; cost – £500

- *standard reports* – a range of reports covering workforce statistics, absence, sickness, labour turnover, holiday entitlement, length of service, appraisal review and training data; cost – £700

- *payroll history module* records pay and deduction details period by period; cost – £300

- *SSP module* provides for SSP calculation and recording; cost – £650.

Further modules are available for administering employee loans and for storing selective information on leavers. A word processing and integrated letter writing package is also available to interface with the personnel database.

Radius Ltd
Wykeland House
47 Queen Street
Hull HU1 1UU
Tel: 0482-227181

Software package
Radius Personnel System (minicomputer version)

Number of installations
100 (personnel only, mostly minis; a further 100 integrated payroll and personnel systems).

Company profile
See page 87.

Hardware
The system has been designed to run on the Texas Instruments Business System 300, 600 and 800 series of minicomputers which can be supplied on a turnkey basis.

Software
The cost of the Radius package is £400. The package comes with 12 fixed fields for personnel data and up to 40 further user-defined fields. Reports are achieved by running the Selective Personnel Report which enables the user to select up to 20 different fields for reporting purposes. Reports may be printed according to a standard format or in a format specified by the user.

Other compatible software available from Radius includes a payroll package, PAYPLUS, and a word processing package, TIPE, to generate standard or personalized letters, contracts and other documentation.

United Professional Services
Bristol House
Victoria Street
Bristol BS1 6BY
Tel: 0272-276140

Software package
UPS System 90

Number of installations
Seven

Company profile
The company began in pension fund administration in 1977 and introduced its computerized pension system in 1979. The personnel system was introduced in 1982 and the payroll system in 1983. In addition to ready made software, bureaux, bespoke software and computer sales and service are also offered.

Hardware
System 90 operates on the Texas Instruments range of super-micro and minicomputers, with a multi-user facility of up to 20 or more terminals or PC's on-line and mainframe communications capability. Texas Instruments hardware can be supplied on a turnkey basis.

Software
System 90 software starts at a basic price of £2,750 for a package designed to hold just over 1,000 records. The system incorporates two separate, cross-referenced files: an 'employee file' containing all the information relating to individual employees and an 'organization file' containing information about the structure of the organization, locations, departments, salary grades and job titles. The system is supplied with a master file of standard records and screen formats which can also be tailored to an individual user's requirements at the time of installation or afterwards.

Other features of the system include:

- multiple level password access

- multiple access facilities enabling records to be accessed in many different sequences

- a range of standard reporting facilities and controls covering establishment control, age and service analysis, salary administration and employee record print

- flexible reporting facilities for listing and counting employees in selected classifications and formats for *ad hoc* analysis.

The following range of optional, additional modules is also available:

- report generator

- SSP, absence and sickness administration

- automatic letter production

- salary administration

- recruitment and selection.

Further modules are in the course of development.

System 90 is one of a suite of three inter-related software packages, the others being *System 70* for payroll administration and *System 80* for pensions administration.

The company provides consultancy and installation support services, hardware and software and a bureau-based personnel system for the smaller user.

Universal Computers Ltd (UCL)
23 Paradise Street
London SE16 4QD
Tel: 01-232 1155

Software package
UCL *Universal Personnel System*

Number of installations
New package

Company profile
Formed in 1979, Universal Computers Ltd is the UK distributor of *Ultimate* minicomputer systems. The company offers a range of

standard applications packages, bespoke software, consultancy and hardware support.

Hardware
The system integrates the PICK operating system with minicomputers from such manufacturers as Honeywell and DEC and the company can supply hardware on a turnkey basis. The system is available in various sizes from single user through to 128 terminals at the top end of the range.

Software
The UCL personnel system starts at £8,000.
    Personnel activities assisted by the system include:

- applicant recording and reporting

- employee engagement, transfer and termination

- benefits management

- performance appraisal

- salary administration

- holiday/leave management

- job evaluation

- skills inventory/job requirements analysis

- manpower planning

- career path planning

- organization charting and profiling.

The main features of the system include:

- screens designed to user's requirements

- 'help' screen facilities

- menu-driven system

- standard reports predetermined by the user

- *ad hoc* reporting

- spreadsheet reporting by means of the UPS spreadsheet package

- graphics.

Optional additional software includes:

- integrated word processing

- SSP/payroll system

- payroll communications module to enable the user to interface with the existing payroll system.

The Wyatt Company (UK) Ltd
Park Gate
21 Tothill Street
London SW1H 9LL
Tel: 01-222 8033

Software package
ABACUS

Number of installations
60

Company profile
See page 89.

Hardware

ABACUS has been designed to run on a PRIME 2250 minicomputer or on any larger minicomputer in the PRIME 50 series range and can be supplied as a turnkey system fully-installed on a PRIME 2250 minicomputer. *ABACUS* is being developed to run on an IBM PC and is also available as an on-line bureau application (see pages 89 and 135 for further information).

Software

ABACUS is an integrated suite of software packages covering personnel, pensions, payroll and the administration profit-sharing schemes which can be purchased as an integrated system or as separate packages. The costs of these packages are available on application to the company.

The personnel system maintains and updates records for each employee covering:

- personal details

- employer profile

- job profile

- skill profile

- work history

- salary history

- absence control.

Other features of the system include:

- personalized letters

- standard reports

- other non-standard or *ad hoc* reports prepared by the user

- word processing

- multiple level password access

- audit trail identifying all changes made to the database.

Optional additional modules include:

- manpower planning

- recruitment and selection

- training and career development

- organization charting

- salary modelling

- job evaluation

- communication facility with Wyatt's Remuneration Data Service (for further details see page 135).

Mainframe computer systems

IBM United Kingdom Ltd
Information Network Services
389 Chiswick High Road
London W4 4AL
Tel: 01-995 1441

Software package
ASPIC (Application System Personnel Information Centre)

Number of installations
A large number of users of AS/*ASPIC* worldwide

Company profile
IBM is the world's leading manufacturer and distributor of computers
and electronic office equipment and provider of associated support
services. Information Network Services is the business unit of IBM
providing a wide range of information and support services to user
organizations.

Hardware
ASPIC has been designed to run on IBM 4300 series mainframe computers with a suitable operating environment for AS. A number of
hardware options are offered. Firstly, via IBM bureau computers, the
system may be accessed from dial-up or leased-line computer screens
in the customer's office (see page 132). The bureau approach can also
be used by customers to evaluate AS and *ASPIC* before installing the

systems in-house. The second option is to run the systems on a dedicated IBM 4300 series computer installed on the customer's premises, linked by leased line to the IBM (Information Network Services) computer centre and operated remotely by IBM. The third choice is to install the system on the customer's in-house computer installation (provided that this has a suitable operating environment for AS), installed and operated by the customer's own data processing department.

Software

ASPIC is one of a range of products written in IBM's Application System (AS), a computer language specially written for the non-expert professional business user. The package therefore consists of two products: AS, general purpose software with a range of business applications, and *ASPIC*, geared to the specific needs of the personnel function.

ASPIC consists of a suite of four software modules:

* employee records maintenance module

* monthly payroll module

* SSP/absence recording module

* pensions administration module.

The basic employee records module provides the facility to store such information as:

* personal data

* education and qualifications

* job and work location details

* pay and benefits details

* job performance.

Some of the applications of the system include:

- manpower planning

- salary planning

- job placement, recruitment and selection

- training administration

- attrition and headcount monitoring

- analysis of leavers

- lateness and discipline monitoring

- health and safety monitoring

- relocation

- redeployment and redundancy

- career planning.

The system incorporates a range of standard reports that are already formatted, but may also be altered, covering: employee profiles, lists and analyses of leavers, headcount/earnings summaries, internal telephone directory, employees due to retire, lists of trades union membership and others. The system also has extensive reporting, text processing and graphics facilities so that information can be presented in a variety of formats including line and surface graphs, bar charts and pie charts.

The prices of these software packages are available on application to IBM.

International Computers Ltd (ICL)
Personnel and Payroll Applications Products
Cavendish Road
Stevenage SG1 2DY
Tel: 0438-313361

Software package
Personnel 29

Number of installations
New package: field trialled in six organizations

Company profile
See page 73.

Hardware
Personnel 29 is designed to run on ICL's System 29 mainframe computer under the VME operating system. The system may be used either as a central installation, as a distributed network or in conjunction with the ICL *Personnel 20* microcomputer system (see page 73).

Software
Personnel 29 is a flexible software package which is modified to the specifications of the user following initial discussions and evaluation involving ICL consultants and the client organization. Following this, ICL presents a detailed proposal outlining the hardware, software, consultancy and training needed to implement the system, together with a cost breakdown and a planned implementation schedule.

Typical applications of the system include:

- recruitment and selection monitoring

- equal opportunity monitoring

- job/post administration

- job description details

- appraisal results recording

121

- promotion eligibility

- government reporting

- pay modelling

- benefits

- incentive schemes

- selection of training candidates

- manpower planning

- information for negotiations

- absence recording

- holidays

- transfers

- education and training

- retirement.

The main features of the system include:

- *ad hoc* reporting facility, using ICL's *Querymaster* software

- standard reports defined by the user, using ICL's *Reportmaster* software

- integrated letter writing, using ICL word processing software

- multi-level password system defined by the user

- audit trail for monitoring who is accessing the system.

Further details on the prices of the hardware and software for running *Personnel 29* may be obtained on application to ICL.

McCormack and Dodge Ltd
PO Box 273
1 Redcliff Street
Bristol BS99 7AL
Tel: 0272-276866

Software package
HR: Millenium (Human Resource Information System)

Number of installations
Four

Company profile
An American company founded in 1969, McCormack and Dodge is part of the Dun and Bradstreet Corporation. As specialists in applications software, McCormack and Dodge's product range is based upon software known as *Millenium* which also forms the basis of their other software products for accountancy and financial applications.

Hardware
HR: Millenium is designed to run on IBM mainframe computers which can be installed and maintained as part of a turnkey arrangement. The McCormack and Dodge *Interactive PC Link* option enables the system to be linked to compatible microcomputers, enabling data to be downloaded from the mainframe without tying up valuable mainframe resources. *PC Link* incorporates graphics options, including bar and pie charts and spreadsheet facilities for 'what if?' analysis.

Software
HR: Millenium is an integrated personnel and payroll package and costs £50,000. The package includes:

- a payroll processing system

- a payroll reporting and payroll history system

- a personnel record and reporting system

- optional additional personnel modules.

Features of the basic personnel module, which can be tailored to suit the needs of the user organization, include the following:

- *general personnel data* – personal data about employees which can be used to analyse employee names by department, generate telephone lists etc

- *promotion/transfer data* contains the education, skills, qualifications, performance and career history of individuals, useful for internal recruitment procedures, performance review reports and career planning and counselling

- *training data*, used in conjunction with the above, for identifying training needs, internal vacancy filling and training course attendance monitoring

- *job data* includes such information as job title, salary, location, supervisor etc

- *wage/salary data* contains detailed salary information for each employee with associated salary reporting facilities

- *illness/injury data* enables analysis of causes by reason and calculation of working time lost

- *workforce analysis* applicable to equal opportunity monitoring

- *personnel profiles* enable the visual presentation of employee data.

The additional optional modules include:

- a 'benefits reporting' module for monitoring and reporting on employee benefits and their costs

- a 'position control' module for keeping track of vacant and filled positions in an organization

- an 'applicant flow' module for monitoring recruitment applications

- a 'safety reporting' module compiling information and statistics on health and safety.

Package Programs Ltd (PPL)
91 Blackfriars Road
London SE1 8HW
Tel: 01-633 0121

Software package
PPL-Cyborg Personnel and Human Resource System

Number of installations
70

Company profile
PPL was established in 1970 by a leading data processing consultancy firm to market packaged application software and is now a leading supplier of application software in the UK. Apart from mainframe software applications packages, PPL has an approved IBM dealership for microcomputers and markets a range of micro software.

Hardware
The *PPL-Cyborg System* is a mainframe package available for a range of installations, including: IBM, ICL 2900 series/VME (except ME29), UNIVAC 1106/08/10, DEC/VAX, Honeywell DPS8 and others.

Software

The *PPL-Cyborg* package is an integrated human resource, payroll and pensions administration system, although any one of these modules may be purchased and used separately. The starting price for the complete package is £20,000 depending on the number of employees and the price includes training, documentation, implementation assistance and the first year's maintenance/support.

The Personnel and Human Resource module provides for the commonly required information needs of the personnel function, with flexibility for the user to tailor and supplement these facilities to meet individual requirements.

Data are held at an 'organization level' and 'employee level'. 'Organization level' files contain data on jobs, establishments, salary data and information for staff budgetting; 'employee level' data include information on employees' personal data, time and attendance recording, skills and education, salaries, jobs, employee benefits and medical information.

Other features of the system include:

- access to data controlled by three password levels (which can be further extended)

- applicant tracking system for controlling and analysing internal and external job applicants

- integrated letter writing tailored to the user's requirements

- diary facilities to remind users of future events and the associated action necessary

- standard and *ad hoc* reporting facilities

- automatic calculations

- facilities for communications links with other systems

- links if required to the *PPL-Cyborg* payroll and pensions systems.

Peterborough Software (UK) Ltd
Borough House
Newark Road
Peterborough PE1 5YJ
Tel: 0733-41010

Software package
UNIPERSONNEL

Number of installations
85 in the UK; 100 worldwide

Company profile
Established in 1963 as Peterborough Data Processing Services, Peterborough Software specializes in the marketing, support and maintenance of mainframe software products for human resource management. Peterborough Software operates from eight countries in the British Isles, Australasia, South Africa and the Far East.

Hardware
UNIPERSONNEL is designed to run on IBM, IBM plug-compatible and ICL mainframe installations.

Software
Peterborough Software supply three packages: *UNIPERSONNEL* (personnel management), *UNIPAY* (payroll administration) and *UNIPENSION* (pensions administration). These may be used as a single integrated system or as separate systems. Peterborough software is not sold to clients but is made available on a rental basis only. Costs are based on the number of employees in the customer organization and further information about these is obtainable on application to Peterborough Software.

The personnel package includes the common data requirements of personnel departments together with a 'parameter file' enabling users to determine what information is held by the system, how it is processed and how the results should be formatted. Thus, periodic changes can be effected without re-programming.

Other features of the system include:

• real-time validation of data entry and update

- standard reporting to a format determined by the user

- *ad hoc* enquiry and reporting facilities

- multiple-level password access

- audit reports monitoring who is entering information, what, when and via which terminal.

Plessey Management Services Ltd
Abbey Works
Titchfield
Fareham PO14 4QA
Tel: 0329-43031

Software package
PREFECT personnel management system

Number of installations
New package: operates at two sites within Plessey

Company profile
Plessey Management Services is a member of the Plessey Group of Companies and operates as a software house serving the computing needs of both the Plessey Company and other major UK organizations.

Hardware
The *PREFECT* is currently available to run on the Digital Equipment Corporation (DEC) VAX mainframe computer under the VMS Version 3 operating system using VT100/VT200 or compatible terminals (VT125 or VT240/1 for graphics).

Software
PREFECT has been developed in conjunction with the Plessey personnel department and the personnel departments of other organi-

zations. The cost of the package is £9,000, including one day's training and a week's installation support. An annual maintenance support contract is available at 12½% of the purchase price. Plessey sees the system as one run through a company's DP Systems function in conjunction with the personnel function.

The system holds the following employee data:

- personal details

- career history

- previous employment details

- educational and professional qualifications

- absence recording and reporting

- details of training courses attended

- historical data

- departmental details

- grade structure details.

The main features of the system include:

- fully menu-driven screens

- multiple-level password access defined by the personnel executive

- multi-user

- standard and *ad hoc* reporting by means of a report generator, which also produces graphs, bar charts, histograms, pie charts, etc

- facilities to store the parameters needed to produce reports and graphs on a standardized basis

129

- audit trail facilities

- bulk updating facilities

- facilities for links between *PREFECT* and other systems by means of 'Datatrieve'.

Bureaux services

Co-Cam Computer Services (UK) Ltd
89 Kingsway
London WC2B 6RH
Tel: 01-404 5881

Company profile
See page 95.

Bureau service
See page 95.

Comshare Ltd
10 Grosvenor Gardens
London SW1H 0DH
Tel: 01-730 9991

Company profile
See page 69.

Bureau service
See page 97.

IBM United Kingdom Ltd
Information Network Services
389 Chiswick High Road
London W4 4AL
Tel: 01-995 1441

Company profile
See page 118.

Bureau service
See page 118.

LA Computer Services Ltd
17 Lansdowne Road
Croydon CR0 2BX
Tel: 01-680 2400

Company profile
LA was established in 1976 and provides a range of computing services, including ready made and bespoke software, bureau services and turnkey arrangements. LA is an agent for TI and DEC computers.

Bureau service
The LA bureau service is available in full on-line mode with inter-active processing, with microcomputer input and enquiry, or in batch processing mode. Apart from their personnel information system, LA also offers an integrated payroll, personnel, pensions and time scheduling service.

LMR Computer Services
54-70 Moorbridge Road
Maidenhead SL6 8BN
Tel: 0628-37123

Company profile
See page 76.

Bureau service
The LMR personnel system, described in the minicomputer section, is available in on-line interactive and batch processing modes. Customers have the option of transferring from the bureau service to their own in-house machine at a later stage.

MSA (Management Science America) Ltd
MSA House
Cedars Road
Maidenhead SL6 1SA
Tel: 0628-39242

Company profile
Established in 1978, MSA provides bespoke and ready made applications software in the fields of accounting, production and stock control, computer training and bureau services.

Bureau service
The *MSA Real Time Personnel and Payroll System* enables the storage of employee data and the provision of standard reports in such areas as absence, personnel statistics and costs, work schedules and employee benefits. For non-standard reports, a report writer facility enables users to format their own reports. The system also has an interactive forecasting and modelling capability enabling plans on staffing and costs to be projected over any given period and a 'what if?' facility to give alternative solutions. All these options may be reported or shown in any graphical format. There is also the facility to download data into personal computers for desk top processing in the form of spreadsheets, word processing or graphics.

133

RHM Computing Ltd
Joseph Rank House
PO Box 11
Haydens Road
Harlow CM20 1LX
Tel: 0279-26831

Company profile
RHM Computing is the computer bureau division of the Rank Hovis McDougall Group. RHM offers a range of computing services, including mainframe based bureau services and consultancy services to assist in the development of telecommunications and interactive database systems and electronic publishing services including the production of microform and laser printed output.

Bureau service
The bureau based personnel service offers flexibility in the content of each record, incorporating a range of predetermined fields with a facility for users to redefine field descriptions and standard wordings by using a series of tables. Use of numeric codes ensures that sorted information in reports is accurate.

All data are updated on line, but for users of the Unipay payroll system (see page 127), some basic data and salary details can be transferred in bulk at set-up time or on request. The system provides 10 online and 10 batch reports and the user can request additional regular reports and define *ad hoc* reports. The client organization can define and set up the specific level of access allowed to each authorized enquirer. Letters can be printed by laser on company headed paper for selected employees, using data from the files.

The system is based on the *ADABAS* database package and access is by any VDU or PC compatible with an IBM 3270. There is no limit on the number of records nor on the amount of history which can be retained on file. Data from the system can also be downloaded to an IBM PC for direct use by DBase II or Lotus 123 using selected fields. Reports can be laser printed or routed to a local printer. Charges are based on the number of records and the intensity of use.

The Wyatt Company (UK) Ltd
Park Gate
21 Tothill Street
London SW1H 9LL
Tel: 01-222 8033

Company profile
See page 89.

Bureau service
The Wyatt *ABACUS* personnel system, one of four integrated modules covering pensions, payroll and profit-sharing, can be installed in the user's own office by means of a visual display unit and printer connected directly to Wyatt's computer by telephone link. For a fuller description of the Wyatt personnel system, see page 116. All users of the bureau service are automatically given access to the Wyatt Information System, which is an up-to-date information bank containing social security contribution/benefit rates and other relevant information for payroll and pension managers.

Special applications packages

This section contains a listing of a range of applications packages available to assist in specialist areas of personnel work.

Access control and security systems

Cardkey Systems Ltd
23 Stadium Way
Reading RG3 6ER
Tel: 0734-415211

Cardkey Systems, part of the Fairchild Corporation, have been manufacturing and distributing computer based access control and alarm monitoring systems in the UK since 1965. The system involves the positioning of 'Cardkey readers' at doorways and the computer-controlled reader determines whether or not access can be permitted. Cards may also be programmed to restrict entrance into certain rooms or areas or even to particular times of the day. Cardkey entry systems can be linked on-line to a central controller enabling the storing and monitoring of personnel movement and the generation of reports for management information purposes.

Job analysis

BIT Business Information Techniques Ltd
Bradford University Science Park
Bradford BD7 1HR
Tel: 0274-736766

A job analysis package is available as one module in the *Parys* suite of programs developed by BIT Business Information Techniques, an independent commercial company specializing in software development and contract consulting in such fields as office automation, telecommunications and 'expert' systems (see pages 141–43 for descriptions of other elements of the BIT suite of software). The suite of programs is referred to as 'expert systems' since it comes complete with a knowledge base to aid analysis and decision-making in a number of fields of personnel work. All programs are written to run on IBM PC/XT hardware or equivalent with a minimum memory of 512 Kbyte, a 10 Mbyte fixed disk, running under the PC-DOS operating system. The company will advise on the compatibility of the software with other microcomputers and on links with other existing systems.

The job analysis package, the *Parys Jobs Manager*, costs £3,600 for the software. The package has the following features:

- it supports the creation and maintenance of a database of job descriptions and personnel specifications

- it constructs organization charts

- it analyses jobs using an expert 'knowledge base' to produce a detailed definition of job content together with a profile of the personal attributes needed in an employee or candidate for good performance in the job

- it provides facilities for correlating job analyses conducted by a number of individual managers in order to assist in writing a consensus job description and personnel specification.

The other modules in the package are as follows:

- the *Parys Personnel Selector* (£3,600)

- the *Parys Screen-Based Tester* (£3,600)

- the *Parys Performance Monitor* (£1,800).

For descriptions of these modules see pages 141–43.

The complete system is available at the reduced price of £9,450 and the integrated package may be used for such applications as:

- recruitment

- organization design

- internal selection

- appraisal and development

- equal opportunities monitoring

- talent spotting

- psychometric testing

- assessment centre applications.

LMR Computer Services
54-70 Moorbridge Road
Maidenhead SL6 8BN
Tel: 0628-37123

LMR produces a range of general personnel systems known as *ADPM* (see pages 76, 103, 133). LMR also produces *ADSKIL*, a package which may be used either on a stand-alone basis or integrated with their other packages and is available to run on **PRIME** minicomputers. *ADSKIL* is a job analysis package for use in manpower planning, training and development and job evaluation and is available from a cost of £1,500.

The basis of the package is a job profile completed by each job holder specifying on a matrix a range of knowledge and skill elements required for the job. Each element may be weighted on a relative scale using four factors (frequency of use, learning time, importance to the job and complexity of usage). The computer analysis may be used in a number of ways, including the following:

- identification of common skill elements between jobs

- identification of additional skills needed in the light of retraining, redeployment, promotion etc.

- identification of skill profiles of different occupational groups

- provision of skill and knowledge indices for different jobs for job evaluation purposes.

Job evaluation

Baker Davis Ltd
48/49 Block D
Planetary Road
Willenhall WV13 3XR
Tel: 0902-726236

Baker Davis have produced a job evaluation package, *Precision Ranking*, applicable to a variety of job evaluation methods including direct consensus/simple ranking, factor comparison and profiling. The package is designed to run on microcomputers under the MS-DOS operating system, for example the ACT Apricot and IBM PC. The evaluation process is conducted directly through the keyboard and the system stores the results of ratings of various job factors for subsequent recall. A series of reports is produced as output, including a graph plot of the resulting scores for each job. The price of the package depends upon the user's precise needs and is available upon application to Baker Davis.

Manpower planning

Institute of Manpower Studies
Mantell Building
University of Sussex
Falmer
Brighton BN1 9RF
Tel: 0273-686751

The Institute of Manpower Studies, founded in 1970, is an independent, national centre carrying out research and advisory work in the manpower field.

The IMS Models library brings together general purpose computer models which are of value in analysing manpower problems and forecasting. Current models and their prices are as follows:

WASP	£2,500
IMS-WASP	£425
CAMPLAN	£4,000
PROSPECT 2	£5,000
MICROPROSPECT	£525

WASP, available for running on mainframe computers, is a wastage analysis package, analysing cohort or census wastage data by age or length of service. The package will also plot and compare wastage patterns. WASP has a projection module which forecasts the age or length of service structure of a group of staff and projects numbers of leavers and recruits.

IMS-WASP is a version of WASP developed for 16-bit micros operating under MS-DOS or PC-DOS requiring a minimum of 128K (MS-DOS) or 196K (PC-DOS) of store to operate. It contains all the features of the mainframe version.

CAMPLAN, developed at Cambridge University, is a mainframe package for identifying problems in career structures, both in the short and long term, and examining the impact of policy changes. It lends itself to strategic thinking on careers more than to detailed short term forecasting (for which *PROSPECT 2* is more useful).

PROSPECT 2 is a mainframe package similar to *PROSPECT* but much more flexible in the manpower structure it can represent, the types and combinations of flows modelled and the variety of output which can be obtained.

MICROPROSPECT is a version of *PROSPECT 2*, developed for eight-bit micros operating under CP/M. It contains most of the features of *PROSPECT 2*, but is restricted in the size of model it can handle.

Performance appraisal, training and development

BIT Business Information Techniques Ltd
Bradford University Science Park
20-26 Campus Road
Bradford BD7 1HR
Tel: 0274-736766

The *Parys Performance Monitor*, part of the *Parys* microcomputer software suite (see page 137) is a package to aid performance appraisal, training and development, and career and succession planning. Its main features are as follows:

- it supports the development of relevant and consistent employee objectives

- it assists managers in making accurate appraisals related to both job content and personal objectives

- it provides guidance and feedback on training, development and attainment.

Psychometric testing

BIT Business Information Techniques Ltd
Bradford University Science Park
20-26 Campus Road
Bradford BD7 1HR
Tel: 0274-736766

As a module in the *Parys* suite of software, described on page 137, BIT produce the *Parys Screen-Based Tester* at a cost of £3,600, which enables psychometric tests to be administered via a VDU screen. The main features of the system include the following:

- the package incorporates a battery of BIT proprietary tests covering a range of personal attributes, characteristics and skills

- it provides immediate access to test scores

- it provides for the automatic collection of demographic data

- it provides an analysis and graphical presentation of the comparative rankings for a group of candidates against both national and local (organizational) norms.

Psyconsult Ltd
Business and Technology Centre
2 Bessemer Drive
Stevenage 5G1 2DX
Tel: 0438-316561

Psyconsult have a range of software available for most popular business computers for the administration of a wide range of psychometric tests by means of a computer. Programs also incorporate a database of occupational norms against which the data user's candidate can be evaluated. Software is available only to qualified users. The price of software for aptitude testing starts at £100. Software for the 16PF, with a built-in database of norms and further facilities to store local or in-house norms, sells for £650.

Recruitment and selection

BIT Business Information Techniques Ltd
Bradford University Science Park
20-26 Campus Road
Bradford BD7 1HR
Tel: 0274-736766

The *Parys Personnel Selector*, part of the *Parys* microcomputer software suite (see page 137), is a package providing assessment advice and selection scheduling and control. It includes the following features:

- it advises on assessment methods and criteria for the attributes required to achieve success in a job

- it provides expert assistance in assessing a pool of candidates for short listing

- it provides guidance for interviews and helps in evaluating and recording the results of interviews

- it supports final selection and the associated activities and documentation

- it provides measurement and analysis of the recruitment and selection process.

Hall Associates (UK) Ltd
Stratton House
29E High Street
Camberley GU15 3RB
Tel: 0276-683761

Hall Associates produce a microcomputer package known as *ARC Automated Recruitment Control* at £2,495 for a single-user version and an additional £345 for each additional screen in the multi-user version. *ARC* is available for the IBM PC/XT, ACT Apricot, DEC

Rainbow, Wang PC and other microcomputers operating under CP/
M-80, MP/M-80, CP/M-86, MP/M-86, PC-DOS, MS-DOS, Concurrent CP/M and Turbo-DOS.

Features of *ARC* include:

- menu-driven screens

- automatic letter functions

- automatic updating of candidate records when sending letters

- candidate and vacancy listings and analysis

- progress chasing and status reports

- fast retrieval of candidates stored for future reference

- recruitment source response analysis and lead-time statistics

- various reports for recruitment monitoring purposes.

PEAR Computing Systems Ltd
129 Queens Crescent
London NW5 4HE
Tel: 01-267 7142

PEAR offer a package known as *GRAPPLE* which is a recruitment
administration system starting at £2,950 for the software, with training at £150 per day and annual maintenance at between 10 and 12½
per cent of the system value. PEAR also undertake to tailor the system
to meet individual client needs.

The system can run on VAX/PDP 11 type minicomputers, the
DEC range, IBM PC/XT and any microcomputer running on PC-
DOS, MS-DOS or Apple DOS for smaller users.

Rostering

SIA Computer Services Ltd
Ebury Gate
23 Lower Belgrave Street
London SW1W 0NW
Tel: 01-730 4544

SIA is a software house offering a range of ready made software in addition to bespoke systems development, hardware and bureau services. SIA offer a roster production and costing system known as *WORKPLAN* at the following prices:

- *mainframe version at £25,000* includes installation, four training workshop allocations, hot-line and software support for the first year and four user manuals

- *minicomputer version at £15,000* includes installation, two training workshop allocations, hot-line and software support and two user manuals

- *microcomputer version at £3,900* includes two training workshop allocations, hot-line and software support for the first year and one user manual.

WORKPLAN enables users to perform the following functions:

- to design rosters and related manpower requirements, taking into account cover for leave, sickness and meal breaks

- to store pay details and cost alternative roster patterns

- to store details of rest day patterns, shift restrictions and guaranteed overtime

145

- to ask 'what if?' questions, such as the impact of changes in the working week or variations in the lengths of shifts.

Time and attendance monitoring

Cardkey Systems Ltd
23 Stadium Way
Portman Road
Reading RG3 6ER
Tel: 0734-415211

Cardkey Systems (see also page 136) produce a range of attendance management systems including *PASS 1500* and *PASS 3100*.

PASS 1500 is designed to run on microcomputers with at least 256 Kbytes of computer memory and a 10.6 Megabyte Winchester disk. *PASS 1500* is designed for organizations with up to 1500 employees and can handle up to 16 time and attendance registration terminals of the Cardkey MD100/101/102 type.

PASS 3100 is a minicomputer system requiring 512 Kbytes of computer memory and a 20-Megabyte Winchester disk. It is designed to record the attendance of up to 10,000 employees and can handle up to 64 (expandable to 128) Cardkey attendance terminals.

The systems also provide a range of attendance reports and can be adapted to interface directly with other systems, eg payroll.

John Lambert Associates
Turret House
Turret Lane
Ipswich IP4 1DL
Tel: 0473-52536

John Lambert Associates are suppliers of a system known as *QTAR* (Quintessential Time and Attendance Recording). P&Q Associates also supply the same system (see below).

QTAR is a microcomputer-based time and attendance recording system able to process 2,000 or more employees. The system may also be interfaced with other computers, eg payroll. *QTAR* is designed to run on microcomputers running under the MS-DOS operating system, with a required minimum 512K memory and 5Mb Winchester disk. It is currently implemented on the IBM PC/XT, HP 150 and ACT Apricot Xi. The cost of the software starts at £3,000.

Mitrefinch Ltd
Tower House
Fishergate
York YO1 4UA
Tel: 0904-52995

Mitrefinch supply a package known as *TMS Time and Attendance Management System*. The system is designed to run on a Data General minicomputer, which is recommended for up to 20,000 employees. A microcomputer system to cater for up to 500 employees is about to be launched and will run on the IBM PC/XT. Software for the minicomputer version starts at £9,000; software for the micro version is expected to cost about £4,500.

The system produces a range of attendance reports and can be adapted to interface directly with other systems, eg payroll.

P&Q Associates Ltd
New Hall Farmhouse
Wareside SG12 7SD
Tel: 0920-66588

P&Q Associates are distributors of the *QTAR Time and Attendance Recording System*, described on page 146.

Plantime Ltd
Shakespeare Industrial Estate
Watford WD2 5HD
Tel: 0923-44300

Plantime is part of Group 4 Securitas International and produces a range of time and attendance management systems including:

- *Autocheck,* an access control multi-level security and time recording system, capable of monitoring up to 16,000 cardholders

- *MAPS* (Management Accounts Personnel System), an integrated time and attendance recording and payroll preparation system

- *Plantime 4,* a flexible working hours time attendance recording and reporting system.

Triad Computing Systems Ltd
42 Kingsway
London WC2B 6EX
Tel: 01-831 7211

Triad produce two time and attendance packages known as *TCR* (Time Clock Replacement) and *TAM* (Time Analysis Module) designed to run on the Microdata M8000 minicomputer. The package caters for large numbers of employees and varieties of work patterns and payment periods and reports can be defined by the user on a range of parameters.

Developing a Computerized Personnel System

The management and buyers' guide

David Burns-Windsor

This prestigious report provides for the first time in Britain a detailed survey of the leading computerized personnel packages currently available for all types of computer. It has been prepared by David Burns-Windsor of information technology consultants Brameur Ltd, in conjunction with the Institute of Personnel Management and the Institute of Manpower Studies. The guide contains a wealth of information normally only available through specially-commissioned consultants' reports, including vendor details and the technical specification, description and evaluation of the packages and their costs. The report is intended to assist personnel functions to save time and money in evaluating what is on the market and assist them to make more effective decisions about the system most appropriate to their needs. The report also contains a detailed description, relevant to the needs of personnel managers, of the issues to be taken into account when considering the development of an in-house system.

At a time when computers and a knowledge of computing are rapidly becoming a normal part of every manager's work, this report provides a unique source of information for personnel managers on this subject, not previously available to the non-technical specialist in such a readily digestible form.

Published by the Institute of Manpower Studies
in association with
the Institute of Personnel Management
and Brameur Ltd

approx 200 pp A4 report format
0 85292 370 8 October 1985 £95.00

Available from:
George Philip Services Ltd, P O Box 1, Littlehampton,
West Sussex, BN17 7EN (Tel: 0903 715599 and 717453/4/5),
cheque/PO with order

IPM COMPANY PERSONNEL SERVICE

Advisory service on computers in personnel

Through its national network of independent advisers with backgrounds in computing and personnel, the IPM Company Personnel Service can offer independent assistance in evaluating and selecting the most appropriate system to meet a company's needs and can also assist with the development of software in-house.

For further information contact:

> Mr S C Golding
> Assistant Director
> IPM Personnel Management Services Ltd
> IPM House
> Camp Road
> Wimbledon
> London
> SW19 4UW
> Tel: 01-946 9100